GLENN HODDLE

MY 1998 WORLD CUP STORY

GLENN HODDLE

MY 1998 WORLD CUP STORY

By Glenn Hoddle with David Davies

ANDRE DEUTSCH

First published in Great Britain in 1998 by

André Deutsch Ltd
76 Dean Street
London W1V 5HA

www.vci.co.uk

André Deutsch is a VCI plc company

Editorial consultant: Olivia Blair
Project editor: Nicky Paris
Editorial contributions from: Hal Norman,
Adrian Lowery, Sarah Mulligan, Kerrin Edwards
Page and plate section design: Design 23
Jacket design: Rob Kelland
Production: Rebecca Gee, Alastair Gourlay

Printed and bound by Butler and Tanner, Frome and London

A catalogue record for this book is available from the British Library

ISBN 0 233 99423 8

Jacket photographs: Allsport, Action Plus, Colorsport and Empics.

Dedication

To mum and dad and all my family and
my friend John Gorman.

ACKNOWLEDGEMENTS

My 1998 World Cup Story is the genuine account of England's bid for the biggest prize in football. It begins in the days leading up to our decisive World Cup qualifying match in Rome in October 1997. It ends sadly but in many ways proudly in the aftermath of our momentous clash with Argentina in St Etienne on 30 June 1998.

It is an honest journal of what happened along the way, of why I did what I did, and how those things came about. None of it would have been possible without the England players, both those who made it to France '98 and those who didn't. I thank them and all my staff who were magnificent throughout. One of them, Tim Sonnex, on his first assignment as a doctor with the senior England Team, doubled as our photographer, a role in which he excelled.

The idea for this book was born in conversations involving my adviser and friend, Dennis Roach, and myself. We had the invaluable advice of Alex Fynn as the project got underway. The assistance of Olivia Blair in writing it has been indispensible.

André Deutsch as the publishers have provided the facilities and encouragement to bring it to fruition. I am especially grateful to Nicky Paris who has worked tirelessly to ensure the tight deadline for publication has been met. I would also like to thank Tim Forrester for his guidance and advice.

My 1998 World Cup Story owes a great deal as well to the patience and hard work of Val and Geoff Partridge at home in Rubery, on the outskirts of Birmingham, who completed numerous typing and other tasks for my co-author at incredible speed.

David Davies and myself have completed this diary in venues all over Europe and further afield, and at all hours of the day and night. How David's found the time to do it, and how his family, Susan, Amanda and Caroline, have put up with it, only they know.

My 1998 World Cup Story is the diary of a dream unfulfilled – until the next time.

CONTENTS

PART ONE

CHAPTER 1

ROME–THE END AND THE BEGINNING

11 OCTOBER 1997

Stress. The staple diet of football managers, they say. I don't think I really experienced it, even in my years as a player and a club manager. But I knew it deep inside me during that night in Rome. The date: Saturday 11 October 1997. There were seconds to go in our final World Cup qualifying game, against Italy. I remember thinking: 'We should be winning. Press the fast-forward button.' And I started to sweat profusely, which I rarely do.

I remember Wrighty hitting the post, and me starting to scream at our players who, for virtually the first time in the match, were out of position. Suddenly we'd lost concentration. Now the ball was at the other end. Over came the cross. Christian Vieri's header. Oh no. It must be in. I felt a physical jump in my heart for the first time in my life.

But it wasn't in, although thirty people on the Italian bench to my left were all up, willing that header home, only to see it go agonizingly wide. Their heads were in their hands.

And then the final whistle. The goalless draw we needed. Joy, relief, pride. A victory jig with my coaching staff that was absolutely spontaneous.

England were going to France, to the World Cup Finals.

I always believed we'd make it, from the day I took over, and that we'd do it by winning our qualifying group, even at the expense of the Italians. You see, I believed in our players. I knew they could compete with the very best; perhaps even beat the very best. If I hadn't believed that, I'd never have taken the England job, even though I really wanted it. OK, so I'd have preferred not to have had to tackle our hardest opponents on their home ground, in front of 70,000 highly charged Italian fans, in our last, decisive, qualifying match – even given that history shows England more often than not get better results in October than in May and early June, when players are often shattered after a long season. That's why our 2–0 win in Poland on 31 May had been so important.

But I understood why not everyone shared my optimism. After all, England had underachieved too often. We missed out on America in 1994 altogether; it was the same story in Germany in 1974 and Argentina in 1978. In 1982 we failed to make the last four in Spain, while Maradona single-handedly sent us home from Mexico in 1986 after the quarter-finals. I knew how painful that had been because I'd played that day, in the heat of the Azteca stadium. In fact, only in Italy, in 1990, had we done ourselves justice.

So the match in Rome was the toughest test of my England reign up to that point; the 'cup final of all the cup finals I've faced so far', as I described it to the media. It was the night when a draw or a victory against Italy would guarantee a successful end to the long and tortuous qualifying road via Moldova, Georgia and Poland and ensure England's place in the World Cup Finals. But for this coach, there was added pressure in the build-up to that crunch match in

Rome, very personal and painful pressure at that. My private life was in turmoil. Eighteen years of marriage were coming to an end; like one-in-three couples, I knew things couldn't go on as they were. So there I was preparing England for their biggest match in years, yet I was also preparing myself for separation from Anne, and from my children: fourteen-year-old Zoe, eleven-year-old Zara and Jamie, who's only five. It was the hardest thing I'd ever had to do in my life but I knew it had to be done. When, was another matter, and that question was tormenting my mind. But I couldn't tell anyone, certainly none of my staff; not even John Gorman, whom I'd known since we played together at Spurs. Yes, there was a football job to do and to burden others would have been unfair, but the main reason was that Anne needed to know before anyone else. It was my secret, something I carried alone in the preparation for the biggest match of my life to date.

This time we would be ready for the Italians. In fact, the build-up was almost tranquil in comparison to the previous February when the Italians had come to Wembley. Within an hour of leaving Wembley after that defeat I knew why we'd lost. I knew deep down that had my most experienced players been available, we'd have won it. But on the night part of the spine of my team had been missing – David Seaman, Tony Adams and Teddy Sheringham. Even my captain, Alan Shearer, had been only half-fit. Now, of course, Alan was out altogether, which was a bad blow. But I was totally confident that Ian Wright would never let England down. And David, Tony and Teddy would all be available. The shape of the team would be the same as it had been at Wembley, but the individuals would be different.

I actually knew my intended team from the day I announced the squad on Monday 29 September. In the back of my mind I was aware that we didn't have to win the game to win the group, and I knew what I wanted tactically: I was determined that we weren't going to get stretched out and lose our shape as a result. I also knew it would probably be the oldest England team I'd ever selected. Rome had to be the occasion for our experienced players; the youngsters – and we have plenty of them – could come off the bench as and when needed. The balance of the team was absolutely key, too, not to mention cool heads and intelligence in football terms.

The worst injury blow we suffered was losing Les Ferdinand to a stomach problem twenty-four hours before flying out of Luton. (Interestingly, the press knew minutes after I did because Steven Howard and Brian Woolnough of the *Sun* were on the phone immediately. Good for them and their contacts, but not necessarily what I wanted or needed.)

The players were told who was in and who was out four days before the match, even before we left England in fact. Thankfully, it made no difference to the atmosphere, which it sometimes does when the team is revealed. I took aside players like Gary Neville and Paul Scholes, who might have expected to play on merit, and told them they had to miss out this time. I didn't want them to think it had anything to do with their performances. Their reaction was typical and terrific. I've actually found it easier leaving players out at international level than I ever did as a club manager. Generally, they understand and accept the tactical reasons behind their omission. I always try to choose my moments to talk to them privately as well, generally quiet times at the team hotel. That's my way of doing things. These are top players and they deserve to be treated as such.

Finding out my teams in advance has been a bit of a media sport in itself. I accept it's fair game – every England manager goes through it – which was why I didn't complain when there was an obvious leak of the team before the game at Wembley against Italy. Matt Le Tissier got most of the blame for that after his brother went public on a local radio station in the Channel Islands to talk about Matt's 'good news'! The other players even gave Matt some stick for apparently being the source of the leak, but I soon knew the original source was elsewhere. Who? That would be telling.

This time, however, I was determined to do everything possible to keep the Italian coach, Cesare Maldini, guessing, even if that meant exaggerating one or two of our injury problems.

Keeping the opposition guessing for as long as possible does help the cause. It's all part of modern football. Of course the Italians – who aren't the only ones – are past-masters at this kind of thing. Indeed, on the day of the match in Rome, RAI (Italian Radio and Television) announced their 'team' six hours before the kick-off and it contained three players – including Attilio Lombardo – who were to play absolutely no part in the actual game. To nobody's surprise, there was the future manager of Crystal Palace in jacket and tie in the stadium lounge, half an hour before the kick-off.

Consequently, we did ask the sports editors of the leading papers to help us by publishing a few either/ors in their probable England teams on the day of the match. We knew this would get back to the Italians since the revelation of our team to the English press before the game at Wembley went straight back to the Italian team hotel via Italian journalists.

All this went through my head as I tried to relax on the flight to Rome, just over seventy-two hours before the match. Skimming the papers, I glanced at the astrology page of the *Express* – you won't be surprised to know I have some faith in astrologers – and in particular at what the stars predicted for a Scorpio (my birthday is 27 October). It told me that 'the situation at home is now moving through a turning point where you will gradually sense a more contented atmosphere. It will be nothing spectacular, but you will be aware of the shift from now onwards. There will no doubt be the odd upheaval in days to come, since you are moving slowly but surely on to a new emotional base'.

Incredibly, it was 100 per cent spot on, since I had already decided that my own personal crisis would come to a head within hours of my return to England.

In Rome I had to be what I demanded of my players when I left the privacy of my bedroom at our training camp, La Borghesiana, and that was absolutely focused on the immediate football task. In the privacy of that room I spent a lot of time on the phone back to England talking to family and friends. I thought about Anne and the children a lot, worrying about them and about the impact on their lives of what I was about to do. The worst times were the mornings when I had to leave my problems behind as we completed our training sessions. I think only John Gorman, who knows me better than anyone else in football, might have suspected all was not well.

Despite all this I slept surprisingly deeply – seven or eight hours a night, regardless of the efforts of our guard dogs who seemed to reserve their loudest barking for my end of La Borghesiana – and in general our preparation could hardly have gone better.

I'd settled on Paul Ince as my captain for the match. I knew the press would be surprised, shocked even, that I didn't go with Tony Adams, but Tony was only recently back from injury and I reckoned the captaincy would be an added burden. He would have wanted the job though, and took my decision like the professional that he is. Incey, meanwhile, was cock-a-hoop. Right from the start of my time in charge I'd seriously considered him for the role permanently, and I knew this game – back on familiar territory for him – would suit him down to the ground.

Yet as little as forty-eight hours before the match he was in a terrible state. I think the cause of his stomach problems was that he wasn't drinking enough water, and I helped him myself with what's known as an 'osteopathic massage' on his stomach area. It's a technique I learned during my time in Monaco from their club osteopath, and is designed to make the kidneys and the liver work more efficiently. It makes you feel fantastic.

Our build-up in the media was refreshingly smooth and

positive. On six days out of nine there were news conferences to attend, and an ever-increasing barrage of questions to answer. My voice suffered as a result. But in Italy we had the inspired idea of asking the former Inter Milan manager Roy Hodgson to act as our interpreter. I was worried he might find the job somewhat beneath him, but as it turned out he loved it and was a huge help in communicating with the Italian media in particular.

'Take no risks' was our policy with the media, which was why Gazza didn't speak to them in Rome as we had anticipated. There was a vague threat that an Italian photographer, with whom he'd had a row during his Lazio days – as I recall it involved a scuffle outside a restaurant – might try to serve an injunction on him. Predictably, it didn't happen but we didn't want to risk even the possibility of any incident, least of all in public.

The criticism again surfaced, especially in the Italian press, that England press conferences were too organized, too controlled, too bland. But we were all too aware of what had happened in the past. Conferences had dragged on and on and the man in charge had lost any control. Graham Taylor – and some of his observations about Gazza's off-the-field activities – provided a legendary example of what can happen. This England coach was determined to stay in control.

La Borghesiana was the perfect place to complete the relaxing build-up we needed. Situated just forty-five minutes outside Rome in its own spacious grounds, it provided the ideal working environment for a football team with a mission. The rooms were sufficient without being luxurious and the surroundings were a world away from the hubbub that would have engulfed us in the middle of the Italian capital. Everything was on hand: training pitches, medical facilities, games rooms and excellent dining facilities, and the security couldn't have been better. I was honestly surprised by how much work we got done once we'd arrived in Italy. The relaxed but determined mood of the staff was obvious.

On the day before the game we trained in the Olympic Stadium. We'd almost completed our work already at a closed morning session at the camp. Now I kept Gareth Southgate out of the action, even though his thigh problem was going to be OK. And I deliberately pulled David Beckham off ten minutes from the end and sent him back to the dressing room with Doc Crane. Did the Italians notice? You bet they did. What did they make of it? I don't know. Call them mind games if you like; if they increased the uncertainty over my team just a tiny bit, they were worthwhile.

Match day dawned warm and sunny. Again I'd slept well despite the best efforts of those guard dogs. We had the lightest of training sessions in the morning and with our pre-match work finally complete, I could even enjoy some lunchtime 'head tennis' with my staff. It was Gorman and Roeder v Hoddle and Clemence, and was to be the only contest I lost that day. No wonder Clem was a keeper – we must remember to work on his first touch for the summer!

At lunch I saw Gazza in the queue. He looked uptight, and that wasn't how I wanted him. But this was his old stamping ground of Rome where he had so many ups and downs with Lazio and where he desperately wanted to do well. I told him he'd be fine, and then said: 'At the end of the day it's only a game, Gazza.' He looked at me astonished. It was the last thing he'd expected from the England coach. But it was helpful to him so it was helpful to me, too.

Some days, you need players to calm down; if they're too hyped up, they don't perform. Others can be too laid-back and need spicing up. Dan Petrescu was like that when I was at Chelsea. I can promise you we'll be trying to relax him if ever we play Romania in the future.

After all the preparation, a long speech from me was the last thing the players needed, so that day's team meeting was the shortest I can remember in my career. It lasted little more than three minutes. All we needed was to believe we were going to get the necessary result, and be sure we were mentally focused. We did, and we were. In fact, only one thing worried me: could we avoid somebody, somewhere, losing his cool and keep all eleven players on the pitch? I made it clear who I thought were the players most at risk – Becks, Wrighty, Graeme Le Saux and Gazza – and I'm sure that saying what I did made them think. It certainly did the trick. How ironic that it was to be the Italians who were to find themselves down to ten men as it turned out. I also told my players I thought they'd win. And I really did.

The journey to the stadium wasn't what we expected. I like to arrive with the team around an hour and fifteen minutes before kick-off. Thanks to two wonderfully aggressive police motorcyclists clearing our path on the highways outside Rome, I was forced to ask our driver to slow down.

Supporters often wonder what it's like on board a team bus bound for a game. Well, that night it was surprisingly quiet. There were the usual card schools, a bit of banter about the music playing, but mostly a lot of silence. You couldn't help but notice the most splendid Roman sunset as we approached the city, and it was at this moment that I sensed it might be a glorious night.

Both John Gorman and I dropped off, but only briefly. We'd specially prepared two videos to play on the coach. One reminded the players of the great England footballing tradition they were following – World Cup '66, Euro '96, and legendary players like Bobby Moore, Gordon Banks, Bobby Charlton and Geoff Hurst. The other reminded them just how good they were – each and every one of them who'd brought England to the brink of World Cup qualification. I remember some of the pictures had been cut to the music of the M People track, 'Search For The Hero Inside Yourself'. It made me shiver with excitement.

As we came closer to the stadium I was astonished by the

number of English supporters. Their numbers grew round every corner and their reception was ecstatic. There were flags, banners, chanting – but most memorably faces, both male and female. It certainly increased our resolve. We wanted to win for them and for our country. Little did we know how depressing an evening it was to be for so many of them, despite our exploits on the pitch.

Once inside the Olympic Stadium, what strikes you underneath the vast main tribune is how far the dressing rooms are from the tunnel and stairway from which the players emerge. Then wallop, the din hits you as you come out on to the pitch. We told the players to warm up at the end where most of our fans were gathered. John Gorman had come up with the idea. Fans and players can gee each other up and they certainly did that night. We had witnessed it at Le Tournoi in France the previous summer, and it worked again.

With kick-off barely fifteen minutes away, my confidence was reinforced. In the players' eyes I could see they shared my confidence, and a determination to do the business. In fact, all us staff noticed it as we changed in our separate area just off the players' dressing room. It was a look that had been missing all those months ago at Wembley before the game with Poland that we almost made a mess of. It was there that night in Rome.

My captain, Incey, seemed more hyped up than usual. I think he was anxious and tense, and desperate to do well. I told him: 'I've got a great feeling. It's going to be a great night for us.'

They tell me my opposite number, Cesare Maldini, could be found staring into space on a little balcony by the side of the Italian dressing room. People have different ways of preparing for their destiny. 'Goodbye in Rome' he'd said to me in Nantes back in the summer when we'd beaten Italy 2–0 in Le Tournoi. We were about to find out if he was right.

The game itself made me very proud of my players, every

single one of them. For long periods we were in control. We were creating the better chances. We were ready for just about everything, even the slightly changed role from what we'd expected of Gianfranco Zola, whose goal had beaten us at Wembley. Zola was the player who'd worried me most before the game. Watching Italy warm up with two strikers – Filippo Inzaghi and Christian Vieri – as well as Zola, I thought they'd probably play Zola in a withdrawn role behind the front two so we pre-empted this just before kick-off with a plan to play David Batty deeper to nullify Zola, with Ince and Gazza tucked in either side. As it turned out we were delighted to see Zola playing wide on the left, as that suited us down to the ground. The players reacted immediately. Experienced players can adapt like that; a young player might have been too concerned about his own performance.

The worst minutes of those ninety for me came during the first half when we were down to ten men. Paul Ince needed stitches as blood poured from his head after he clashed in mid-air with Demetrio Albertini, and I have to admit I lost my rag briefly and gave a rollicking to Doc Crane, our medical man. John Crane is a highly respected doctor who's served a succession of England coaches. But in the heat of the moment I didn't think he realized the urgency of the situation.

Incey had to be led to the dressing room – a good 300 yards away, I'd say, plus up and down a good few stairs – and unbeknown to me at the time, when he got there with the Doc and our physio Gary Lewin, the door was locked. Who had the key? Our Italian hosts around the dressing room obviously couldn't help... so Gary had to sprint back to the bench, then back to the dressing room again before they finally got in to give Incey the stitches in his wound.

That will never happen again. We learned our lesson. We must be able to stitch people by the side of the pitch if necessary.

Meanwhile, despite some choice language from me, the players were coping very well. Teddy Sheringham had dropped deeper and we were managing to keep possession. It was actually one of our best periods. But going seven minutes or more without putting on a substitute, perhaps Nicky Butt, was a risk. Because of the distance to the dressing room I was never really sure what was happening back there. But Incey had told me he'd be OK, and he was.

Throughout the game, and especially during the first half, I was conscious of the crowd problems that led to so much controversy afterwards. Of course I was anxious about their impact. I had friends in that crowd who'd travelled over from England. Only later did their stories confirm the over-reaction of the Italian police, and the mistreatment of so many of our supporters.

All I remember during the game, though, is saying a quick prayer that things would calm down. I believe in the power of prayer because I've seen it work in my life. It was the right thing at the right time, although I pray every day, whatever the situation.

The end of the match couldn't come quick enough, although those final few minutes when Wrighty hit the post and Vieri's header flew wide seemed to pass in slow motion. David Seaman told me afterwards he always knew that header was safe. Thanks David! It shows how different the view from the bench can be from the view on the pitch.

When the final whistle went John Gorman and Ray Clemence, especially, were absolutely delirious. I wanted to shake hands with Cesare Maldini as I'd done at Wembley. Now our roles were reversed. He it was who faced the unpredictable, backdoor route to France via the play-offs (and as it turned out, the snows of Moscow). But he was buried beneath the cameras and microphones. Such is the Italian way: organized (I assume) chaos, very different to what I like.

I'm still waiting for that handshake. All I remember is Gianfranco Zola saying simply, 'You deserved it.' I valued that.

The players celebrated in their own ways. Wrighty was in

tears. 'I'd have shot myself if Vieri had scored after I'd hit the post,' he kept repeating, and at that moment he probably meant it. Gazza and Incey were milking the adulation of the fans. But Tony Adams was different, preferring to stand alone in the middle of the pitch taking in this moment of triumph. David Seaman of all people admitted he'd never been so nervous about any match.

But it was over and we'd qualified, and at that moment the thought crossed my mind that if it was like this now, just imagine what it could be like in France...

In the long tunnel I bumped into Incey mid-interview. I embraced him and he tried to involve me in his answers. 'No, you did the job,' I said, and ran on. Once alone, I said another prayer – of thanks.

During the most enjoyable press conference of my England reign, I talked and talked while the hunt was on – unsuccessfully as it turned out – for champagne for the dressing room. We'd taken nothing for granted by bringing it with us. Afterwards I went into the Dutch referee's room to congratulate him. I'd have done so whatever the result. On a night like that, we needed a good but strong referee. That's always important in a tight game. In my eyes he'd been out-standing, and you never know when we might see him again.

The night was young, but for me the best was over. Our departure from the stadium was delayed by F.A. staff being forced to stay behind to try to get our fans let out of the ground. Even my own videoman, Gary Guyan, who records every game from the camera position I want, was stranded. Our international administration assistant Michelle Farrer had gone back into the stadium to see what was going on. The players were anxious to get going until I pointed out that she was still inside. They weren't going to leave her behind so we waited, but by the time we boarded the plane, the early arrivals among the journalists had been there a while. Predictably they'd drunk the plane dry of beer!

There was a sense of elation on board the flight home, a sense of something achieved together. But I think one or two people noticed how quiet I was. It was nothing to do with football of course. Reality had dawned on me. Achieving the result we needed in Rome was nothing compared to the challenge I now faced at home.

Finally I pulled myself together, and even started talking to John, Clem and Glenn Roeder about the prospects for France. Then, at precisely 4.40 a.m. on a wet Sunday morning, we arrived back at Luton airport. The players, tired but jubilant, dispersed, but we had to face yet another press conference before running the gauntlet of the welcoming party of cameras and fans.

Eventually, and not without difficulty, I found Ray Cousins, a family friend who was driving me and John Gorman home. And at last, in the tranquillity of the car, I could sleep. I don't remember dreaming of anything, just feeling satisfied that we had done what we had set out to do.

Ray woke me up as we pulled into my front drive. Anne had had friends round to watch the match with her but it was now 6 a.m. and I knew she and the children would be asleep. The house was silent.

Suddenly, back in England and at home, all that had gone on in Rome meant rather less. Suddenly, I didn't feel like the England coach who'd conquered Rome. In fact, triumphant was the last thing I felt; though what it would have been like if we'd lost on top of everything else just doesn't bear thinking about.

Within twenty-four hours there was something very different to be done – that of explaining to Anne and the children that I was leaving, and telling them why as best I could. A chapter in my life would be coming to an end and for once, football couldn't help me. I felt alone. I was alone.

CHAPTER 2

HOPES AND FEARS

NOVEMBER 1997 – FEBRUARY 1998

On that night in Rome, there were just 242 days to go until the World Cup Finals would begin. The euphoria was to last until Christmas, but not beyond. My task was to ignore the hype and get it right in June. My problems had begun much earlier, back on 1 May 1996 when I was appointed. I wasn't made particularly welcome by the then England regime during Euro '96 when I was waiting to take over from Terry Venables. The F.A. might have done more to help – perhaps they should have insisted I was allowed some involvement with players whom I was soon expected to take to the World Cup Finals – but Terry made it clear he didn't want me around during Euro '96, except for one short visit.

I've never really got close to Terry, despite working with him on ITV. A few of the things he's said about England since I took over have irritated me. Perhaps that's inevitable. He isn't aware of it and I've chosen not to tell him.

I don't think managers should make life more difficult than it already is for their successors. I certainly haven't gone on about how the foundations of Chelsea's present team were laid in my time as manager, since I left Stamford Bridge. I've definitely learned a lesson in how to handle myself when the time comes to hand over the England reins.

Of course, that's a long way off now I hope, whereas France '98, is not. On 4 December, the scheduled date of the draw in Marseilles, we would know the identity of our first-round opponents in France. But before all that I had unfinished business at home to sort out.

I was determined details of my personal turmoil shouldn't trickle into the press when I wasn't ready to handle it. So less than seventy-two hours after returning from Rome I broke the news of my marriage break-up, first to John Gorman, and then to The F.A.'s Public Affairs Director, David Davies.

I'd told John on several occasions that there was something on my mind that he needed to know about. He knew it wasn't a football matter, and I now know he'd suspected it was about my relationship with Anne; he'd noticed that things seemed to have changed. The fact that he'd even mentioned it to his wife Myra just shows how well he had got to know me.

David was very shocked, despite the fact that he had always been concerned about the impact of the job on someone with a young family. He immediately issued a short statement on my behalf. It read: 'The England coach, Glenn Hoddle, wishes it to be known that with great sadness he has separated from his wife Anne. This is a personal and private matter. It is unconnected to his football responsibilities. Nobody else is involved. Both Anne and Glenn would request that the privacy of themselves and of their children is respected at this very difficult and painful time.'

I knew the likely reaction, and so did those closest to me. Our house was besieged, and even though the whole family had temporarily moved out – I was dividing my time between friends such as Phil and Eileen Drewery and John and Myra Gorman – it still didn't take the press long to track down both Anne and me. As you can imagine there were some lively exchanges with photographers, some of whom almost literally lived on our doorsteps for several days. You have to experience it to know how awful it is. I especially resented the press making contact with school friends of my children, because naturally I worried about them most of all. But as I'd said from the start, nobody else was involved. And within forty-eight hours I was back at Lancaster Gate trying as best I could to get on with my life.

We quickly confirmed a fixture with Cameroon at Wembley for 15 November. It was to be the same day, ironically, as the Italians finally qualified for France with the narrowest of victories over Russia in Naples. I'm sure Cesare Maldini would have gladly changed places with me that day.

The Cameroon game was just about my first time at Wembley when I wasn't under the pressure of a truly competitive and vital match, and I got the result and the performance I wanted. It was not, as some of the media had suggested, an anti-climax after the drama of Rome; in fact, the crowd of almost 47,000 was terrific for a friendly match.

Paul Scholes and Robbie Fowler got the winning goals; Gazza had a good game; and Andy Hinchcliffe and Rio Ferdinand both enhanced their reputations. The left wing-back position was really still up for grabs then. There aren't too many naturally left-sided English players currently in the game and I was looking for someone who was sound defensively but who could also give us an edge going forward. Andy did both, which was encouraging. Rio's debut, as a substitute, was a really accomplished one. His calmness on the ball made a difference to the game, and although he'd still got things to learn defensively, he was certainly a long shot for France.

Cameroon, as I'd expected, were inventive opponents. They passed the ball well and had considerable vision. But they were also raw, and their teamwork was a bit undisciplined. To be honest, I didn't think they'd progressed much from the Cameroon team who'd impressed in the World Cup in Italy seven years ago.

By this time England had moved up to sixth in the official FIFA World Cup rankings, but in advance of the Marseilles draw the controversy was over whether or not we'd be seeded in France. Until the last moment we didn't know on what basis the decision would be taken, but as we'd half-feared and expected, performances in previous World Cup Finals – in Mexico, Italy and America – ultimately counted as more important than the rankings. As we'd not even made it to America, our chances of being seeded disappeared.

Actually, it wasn't as much of a blow as it would have been in the days when the seeds had the advantage of playing all three of their group matches at the same venue. But it confirmed my view that England always seem to be fighting against the tide. The rules on seeding weren't even decided until after the qualifying matches had been completed. Beforehand, the issue was simply left hanging in the air. And no offence, Mr Maldini, but in these days of play-offs in the qualifying rounds, surely countries that only make it 'by the back door' shouldn't be seeded?

Even before the draw, however, I'd decided that England would be based at the Hotel Du Golf near La Baule in northern France, regardless of who and where we were to play. It had been our base for Le Tournoi and had worked for us. It provided the seclusion, tranquillity and facilities we needed, and was no more than ninety minutes by plane from any of the designated World Cup venues.

My immediate destination, however, was the south of

France. Marseilles was teeming when I arrived twenty-four hours before the draw, and I was immediately struck by just how huge the World Cup has become. Thirty-two countries were there, and most of them seemed to be represented in numbers in our hotel.

The foyer was in utter chaos when we arrived, and the television camera crews of the world were on red alert, so much so that within minutes of arriving I'd had five phone calls in my room, all asking me for 'just a few questions, Mr Hoddle'. It was like a cattle market.

Before the draw, every delegation was invited to a dinner in one of Marseilles' historic buildings on what must have been the coldest and windiest night in the city's history. The wind was so strong and bitter that there were rumours the draw would have to be staged inside rather than in the open air as planned. I've no idea whether or not they used a seeding system for the tables, but England was allocated a small one in the corner of the room and some distance from the Germans, Italians and French in the centre.

Personally, I don't really enjoy the hobnobbing that goes on at these social events. They are always stiff and formal, and there's too much ego flying around. However, it's all part of the job, and I must admit I enjoyed talking to the other coaches, in particular Germany's Bertie Vogts. He and I compared notes about our respective World Cup preparations, which were remarkably similar. But I thought that the Germans would find the south of France, where they would be based during the Finals, too hot for their liking.

It was also good to meet up again with the Liberia and AC Milan striker George Weah, who I played with at Monaco. We had a natter about the old days and I was pleased to find him still down to earth despite his fame. He seems to be enjoying life in Italy. (Talking of Italy, I still didn't manage to shake hands with Cesare Maldini, despite my best intentions.)

The draw itself, at the Vélodrome stadium in Marseilles,

remained an open-air event – which was a pity considering the awful weather. Still, the idea to kick off with an exhibition match between Europe and the Rest of the World was a good one, even if it went on a bit for a non-competitive game and the crowd got rather restless.

The draw was always going to be a nerve-wracking affair. I was sitting level with the eighteen-yard box so was too far away from the stage to have a decent view. The cameras, meanwhile, had their work cut out trying to catch the various coaches' reactions. I wonder if they panned in on the Romanian coach when England came out of the hat in his group ... his face dropped a mile!

Actually, some of our delegation had had a hunch we'd end up in Germany's group, which might have suited us; at least we'd then have had a chance of avoiding meeting them in the quarter-finals had we both qualified from the same group. As it turned out the Germans got the USA, Yugoslavia and Iran while we were grouped with Romania, Tunisia and Colombia. As the draw wore on I was hoping we'd get Iran instead of Colombia, but no such luck. The Iranians would have suited us better.

'It could have been worse' was my instant reaction to the BBC's Ray Stubbs on a freezing, cramped, chaotic television gantry when it was all over. Actually, it couldn't have been much worse considering our group was the only one containing three teams ranked in the world's top ten. Because of that, on reflection I thought we'd landed in the most difficult group of all. But the English media predictably wrote it up as 'Glenn in Heaven', or something like that, picturing me on huge TV screens in the stadium apparently beaming with satisfaction. To be completely honest, it was the cold.

I'd been warned about what was expected of the England coach by the media after the draw. In international competition these days they have what's called 'the mixed zone' in which coaches and players are supposed to chat to as many journalists as are around. It can be chaotic, but I was pleasantly surprised at how well organized it was in Marseilles. Among the highlights was the Brazilian radio journalist who fired a question at me and then stuck a mobile phone against my ear. Apparently, I was live on Brazilian TV. It wasn't really the one-2-one I'd have chosen!

With the draw done, one of my first priorities was to sort out a fixture list that would ensure we got the preparation we needed before the Finals. Believe it or not, we'd already pencilled in Colombia for February 1998 at Wembley, but even before the draw was over we heard they wanted to call the game off. It didn't bother me as we had a long list of teams who did want to play England, especially at Wembley. In fact, throughout 1997 we'd had numerous requests from countries wanting to play us, home or away, but I didn't want to commit to anything until we'd qualified and knew who our initial opponents in France would be.

But one country, in particular, seemed really keen, and that was Saudi Arabia. I realized just how serious they were when our travel manager, Brian Scott, told me he'd seen an Arab-looking gentleman knocking on my hotel bedroom door in Marseilles while I was out. The written message I received from the Saudis when I got back left me in no doubt.

England had only met Saudi Arabia once before. The game, a 1–1 draw in a friendly in Riyadh in 1988, gave one of my predecessors, Bobby Robson, a problem or two. I didn't play, but I do remember the press urging Bobby to experiment. He did, and the result produced the memorable headline: 'In the name of Allah go!' (Nice business, isn't it?) Of course Bobby stayed and led England to the World Cup semi-finals in Italy less than two years later.

My problem with the Saudis was very different. You see, England's bid to stage the 2006 World Cup was an extra consideration for The F.A., who have to think commercially and politically as well when deciding on 'friendly' fixtures. For that reason the 2006 campaign team, led by Alec McGivan, were keen on the Saudis as opponents, but I wanted to wait and see who we drew in France. Alec, however, had had a meeting in Riyadh three weeks before the Marseilles draw to discuss the 2006 bid with Prince Sultan Bin-Fahd, son of the Saudi ruler King Fahd and deputy president of their Football Federation, and he wanted something positive to offer them.

Unfortunately, his enquiry as to whether they would be available on 23 May 1998 – our last Wembley date before travelling to France – was interpreted as an invitation and was accepted immediately. Of course, once we'd drawn Tunisia in the Finals I was really keen on a game with Saudi Arabia, but my request to bring it forward to one of the international dates earlier in the year almost caused a full-scale row between our two countries. The Saudis didn't believe my request was made for football reasons. They considered it an insult, and the British Embassy staff out there were worried about the impact of this on British – Saudi relations, already strained by the imprisonment of two British nurses on charges of murder over there. Britain and Saudi Arabia also had an agreement to build sporting links that had been developing over the last decade.

Our delegation – who had flown to Riyadh two weeks before Christmas to represent England at meetings while the Confederations Cup was in progress – were met at Riyadh airport both by the Saudis and worried diplomats from the British Embassy at almost midnight. Four hours of meetings followed immediately. There was even the possibility of having to leave Saudi Arabia earlier than planned if the game was cancelled by the Saudis. They wouldn't have been given any souvenirs to bring back either, you could be sure of that. I was phoned at home in the early morning to be told of the seriousness of the situation. I knew immediately that the game had to go ahead on the original date. Eventually our delegation met representatives of the Saudi Federation in one of the magnificent marble offices of the King Fahd Stadium later the following day to confirm the game. A toast was drunk with orange juice. They say it's only about football!

Sir Alf Ramsey's declaration back in 1966 that 'England will win the World Cup' put pressure not just on himself, but on every one of his successors. Now the media wanted me to make the same prediction as Christmas came and went and we moved into World Cup year.

I wouldn't do it. It was the last thing the players would have wanted to hear. It would have lumbered them with the biggest burden of all. But I was aware of the expectations surrounding the World Cup. Too many people seemed to have been seduced by our success in qualifying as winners of a very tough group. In fact, they seemed to believe that we simply had to turn up in France to walk away with football's biggest prize. It wasn't that I didn't want people to believe we could win. I'm all for a positive feeling, particularly when it gets through to the players. But it can go too far.

I'd experienced something similar on a smaller scale when I was player-manager at Swindon. The fans would say, 'You will get us promotion, won't you Glenn?' They said it so often, they expected it as their right. After all, Swindon had won promotion two years before, in 1990, only for it to be denied them due to alleged financial irregularities within the club. The expectation became a burden both for me and the Swindon players.

So with the World Cup Finals now just six months away, we had to somehow strike a balance between getting our preparations spot on on the one hand, and handling the mounting expectation on the other. Mind you, losing a game or two along the way wasn't exactly what we had in mind at the time.

At least I'd had the advantage of experiencing World Cups myself, and of knowing what matters to players, which is why I'd been so keen to appoint a welfare officer to the England set-up. I knew we could learn from others' experiences, too. For instance, the then Brazilian coach Carlos Alberto Parreira (who later took charge of Saudi Arabia) recognized the dangers of negative publicity on his young players and banned newspapers in Brazil's hotel during USA '94. It's so obviously detrimental to a player's state of mind to read damaging headlines and player ratings – regardless of whether they're true, false or somewhere in between – when you need him to be completely focused for the next match. On top of that I believe so many news stories linked to football are either untrue, vastly exaggerated or irrelevant as far as footballers are concerned. But they can still damage our chances of success. Typical, in early 1998, was a *News of the World* story headlined: 'Tony Adams In World Cup Ticket Scam', which then went on to reveal Tony had nothing to do with the story himself.

However, at this time I had more to worry about with Tony Adams than unfounded news stories. His ankle problem notwithstanding, my main concern was Tony's overall fitness: both mental and physical. In the past he's admitted to waking up and not wanting to train, to being negative to the extent of not even knowing if he has – or even wants – a future in the game. Thankfully his mental approach has now changed for the better. But his mind still needs to be stronger. Arsène Wenger and I have both talked to him, but Tony has had to talk to himself to convince himself. I really hoped he would make it to France but I couldn't be sure, and I knew I was going to have to play some friendlies without him to look at possible alternatives.

To lose Tony Adams would have been a big, big blow. Gazza, who I also didn't want to lose, was giving me cause for concern at this time as well. He was not playing regularly for Rangers, and I was still worried about some of his habits and actions off the pitch. Playing that imaginary flute in front of the Celtic fans over the New Year was a bad sign. He knew it, and apologized, but I felt it showed he'd taken a step backwards after his progress in 1997.

I'd bent over backwards to help him in the past, but hadn't seen him for several months when the squad met up for the Chile friendly at Wembley on 11 February, and knew he needed a jolt. We spent an hour talking in my room. He's worth it; his last four games for England in 1997 were terrific and I told him so. Luckily I know how to treat him – with the right mixture of love and discipline.

I believed that Gazza could be as influential as he was eight years ago, but his game has changed. I'm not sure he can go past three players at speed at the top level anymore, but rather by holding the ball he can involve others and still create something special.

It's his mind that's the key; at least 50 per cent of his problems are of his own making. He has to learn to shut out private things, to put them in a box and only open that box at the right time; otherwise they'll sap his energy. If his mental attitude is wrong and he's too negative, he's also more likely to pick up injuries. But I think he's been almost constantly preoccupied with all the problems surrounding his separation from his wife and son. His fitness levels also concern me.

If Gazza had suffered the kind of short, sharp shock at eighteen that Rio Ferdinand had after his drink-driving conviction, then he might not have had half as many problems. But I couldn't kid myself: I knew we weren't out of the woods yet as far as Gazza was concerned and I had to face the fact that I might have to go to France without him. There were only a dozen or so club games left for him to prove that he was ready.

David Beckham, meanwhile, still has to learn not to react, either to referees or to hostile crowds. During Le Tournoi he got himself an unnecessary booking which meant he missed out on playing against Brazil, and I do worry about his reaction to certain situations. Of course, it's a backhanded compliment in many ways – the best players take most of the stick. But he's got to realize that people are jealous of him – he's young, talented, glamorous, and engaged to Victoria, for heaven's sake – and try to put himself in their shoes. They can spend half their wages every week going to football matches and they don't necessarily support his team, so they react accordingly.

Up front I was delighted that Alan Shearer was back, but he needed more games. I was relieved when he got through them. He's still my captain – it's the way he handles himself on and off the pitch that made me go with him as skipper in the first place – and that hasn't changed.

Of course it's a bonus to have players like Tony Adams and Incey to captain the side as well. Going with Incey in Rome was right, then against Chile in February I gave Tony the armband again in a game that gave me the chance to try something new. The press are always delighted by change, unless you lose of course.

At least they weren't short of stories after my squad announcement – Michael Owen became the youngest player this century to play for England. Everybody had been impressed by him on and off the pitch. Talking to the Sunday papers I compared him to Ryan Giggs in terms of the impact he made on me the first time I saw him when he came on as a sub against Wimbledon and scored. He stood out that much. He was doing things some twenty-eight and twenty-nine year olds struggle with, yet he was only seventeen.

Michael's great strengths as a striker are his perception and vision. I don't know if these are natural or taught. If they're taught, he's certainly been listening. With some players, you give them the knowledge but they can't retain it and use it in a game. Michael Owen uses it at absolutely the right time. His pace and his timing together make the difference, especially his ability to run with the ball at pace. He also makes clever runs without the ball.

I think his parents have helped him. He's so level-headed. When we talked to him just before his first Bisham Abbey press conference he seemed already prepared for it. His big tests, though, are still to come, and I'm glad he's got the same agent – Tony Stephens – as Alan Shearer and David Beckham, because as a young player it's vital to have the right people around you. It is easy to forget that footballers are also people. Yes, they are players for ninety minutes once, perhaps twice, a week, but for the rest of the time their lives need organizing like everybody else's.

Michael was the main victim of one of the few press stories that really annoyed me. In talking to a journalist on the telephone – something that I generally avoid – I said that young players like Michael had to be good professionals on and off the pitch. I talked about Rio Ferdinand, Emile Heskey, Richard Wright, Michael Duberry ... and Michael Owen.

This was fairly reported by Henry Winter of the *Daily Telegraph* with whom I had the conversation, but by the time it had been passed on, it had been interpreted as a warning to Michael, who was probably the last person in need of such a message. It was the last time I would ever communicate with the press by telephone.

In some ways it was unfortunate that Michael's big chance came at a time when his team-mate Robbie Fowler had, by his own admission, lost form. I knew people would be surprised when Robbie was excluded from both the senior and 'B' squads against Chile. But I knew what he could do for us; he'd done it against Mexico and Cameroon in 1997 and had nothing to prove at that time. That's what I told him on the telephone.

Two weeks later I had to speak to him again. He deserved much better than the knee ligament injury in the Merseyside derby that ruled him out of all our plans. John Gorman also spoke to him. Such conversations aren't easy, even for John who speaks to players all the time as part of the job I expect of him. I mean, what can you say? Don't worry, you're young enough for another World Cup. The same thing happened to me – I was out for seven months as a youngster at Spurs with an Achilles heel injury. Be patient. Don't rush back. Get yourself right first. Words aren't really enough.

Three or four months had passed since he scored for England and Robbie had been going through a rough period in his club form. The irony for him was that in those two weeks since I'd left him out of the squad he had worked incredibly hard and he had just started to turn the corner. He was almost certain to have been in my next squad. That's how cruel football can be.

Dion Dublin, certainly my surprise choice for the Chile game, knew that. He'd broken a leg after only a few games as a Manchester United player in the early 1990s but his career was reborn at Coventry. I love Dion's attitude. He'd nearly got in the squad a year ago as a defender, and if we were to be limited to twenty-two players in France Dion's versatility would strengthen his case for inclusion.

I thought he did really well on his international debut in that Chile game, but I found it laughable that some of the press compared him afterwards to John Fashanu. They're really different players, and if I'd wanted to waste my time I'd have sat down with some of Dion's critics and explained why.

Actually, it was just a pathetic way of getting at me after England lost. OK, so it was a disappointment, particularly since there were almost 70,000 fans inside Wembley as compared to the last time Chile came to London, in 1989, when the old stadium had had its smallest crowd for an international – just 15,000. But we'd had only seventy-two hours with the players at Bisham Abbey before the game whereas the Chileans had been together for almost two months.

During the match I knew I needed to look at individuals, needed to see them defending in a particular way from the halfway line, but as it turned out our plans went out of the window and the contact between midfield and defence broke down. Too many players forgot their responsibilities and playing Chile turned into a learning experience – if you get stretched out as a team, most opponents will cause you problems. In a nutshell we gave the Chileans, not least Marcelo Salas, too much space, and we paid the price.

I was impressed with Salas. His first goal was right out of the top drawer and I was surprised by how good his first touch was. But we've got one or two who can play a bit, too, and he was no better than any of them.

Still, I had to view the defeat as positive if only that it deflated those high expectations that I warned about at the turn of the year. Who would be worried about the Chile result if we were to beat Tunisia in our first World Cup match in Marseilles?

One person who wouldn't be involved then, nor at any time while I remain national coach, was Chris Sutton. He chose to withdraw from the 'B' squad because he thought it wasn't good enough for him. He told me so in a telephone call. It wasn't a long conversation. I think his manager at Blackburn, Roy Hodgson, tried to persuade him to change his mind, but at least Chris spoke to me himself, and I respect him for that.

But he totally misinterpreted what a 'B' game was about. In contrast to Chris, Paul Merson did himself a great deal of good in that 'B' game against Chile. Chris let himself down and that's the end of it. I really don't need someone around who doesn't want to play for his country. My own fifty-three caps taught me that almost every player wants to play for their country as many times as possible. Just ask those who never got the chance.

When I was Chelsea manager I was always delighted for

players called up on international duty, but not all managers are as accommodating. In recent months, however, I think I've developed good relationships with most top managers. In Alex Ferguson's case, I've had to.

United's success has meant that both he – and his players – have had more demanding club commitments than anybody else, yet he's often had seven or eight players I've needed. We had some lively exchanges on the phone early on, but we've come to an understanding. We got to know each other better working together for ITV during Euro '96, which helped our lines of communication. He's told me he will never let me down, while I've sometimes released injured players early at his request.

Arsène Wenger has been the most helpful manager of all – we've talked regularly about his players, especially Tony Adams and Ian Wright. Of course, it's helped that we've known each other since I played for him at Monaco, but there's a different mentality in France. When players are selected for international duty, there's no debate. They just go.

These days there's a new slant on the old club versus country issue: it's more like English club versus foreign country. There are now so many foreign players in the Premiership that club managers are forever checking the fixture lists of the likes of Uruguay, Jamaica and Australia. And as Middlesbrough found to their cost, losing star names like Juninho and Emerson to international duty in the middle of a season can be devastating. Fortunately for me, the answer must be to develop more English talent.

Here, there's a myth perpetuated by some clubs that players aren't looked after as well with England as with their clubs. But the opposite is true; just ask the players. The fact is, most of England's medical staff come from the clubs themselves. The legendary Dr John Crane has served Arsenal for nearly thirty years and has been involved with England since the days of Bobby Robson and Graham Taylor. Gary Lewin has been Arsenal's physio for years, while clubs queued up for Alan Smith's services as a physio before he joined Terry Venables, and then me, in the England set-up. Steve Slattery, our masseur, was at Swindon with me and Terry Byrne works at Chelsea.

For the record, we were to have two physios, two masseurs and two doctors at the World Cup in order to give the players the best medical support possible. So if there were problems in the past, they don't exist now, and if any club wants to send their own staff to see what we do at first hand they are welcome.

Three months before the World Cup was due to begin John Gorman and I went to Tunis to see our first opponents play Yugoslavia. They lost 0–3 but should have been two up before the Yugoslavs got on top. For half an hour they were pretty impressive. They looked strong defensively as well as going forward but seemed to lack any belief in their ability to score, and eventually fell apart.

It was particularly interesting to see how their fans reacted, considering that the match in Marseilles would be like a home game for Tunisia. Once their team went behind, the fans turned on them. I've never seen that happen so violently anywhere in the world. It would obviously be a huge bonus for us if we could take an early lead against them.

After that trip, not to mention hours spent watching Tunisia and our other opponents on video, I couldn't believe the *Express* journalist who criticized me for not travelling thousands of miles to West Africa to see Tunisia play again, this time in the African Nations Cup. If he had thought for a minute he would have realized that watching our opponents against European opposition was a much more valuable experience. If Tunisia had reached the semi-finals or final of that competition, we'd have been out there like a shot, anyway. That kind of criticism is frustrating, but generally I try not to read things that make me feel negative and wind me up. All that mattered then was that we were on course for France.

Moreover, I was determined not to make the mistake I made at the end of the 1996–7 season when I got sick of watching football. It was while watching a game at Highbury – just a coincidence – that I realized I'd been seeing the same things time and time again. I wasn't learning anything. I was over tired. I simply couldn't afford to let that happen and I needed a break. I'd be no good to anyone, least of all England, if I was shattered in the countdown to the World Cup Finals.

CHAPTER 3

PREPARING RIGHT

MARCH – APRIL 1998

As I gazed out of the coach window on that bitterly cold afternoon in Paris, I suddenly felt really excited … and very, very proud. Around me were my counterparts, and rivals, from all over the world. Nearby sat Brazil's Mario Zagallo, Spain's Javier Clemente, and the French coach Aimé Jacquet. Behind me there was a still distant Cesare Maldini deep in his own thoughts, the Dutchman Guus Hiddink, Scotland's Craig Brown and the Romanian coach Anghel Iordanescu, with whom I shared a bit of banter. His English was pretty good, but my Romanian … well, guess!

Like me, they were all in Paris on 9 March for a so-called 'World Cup Workshop' of the competing nations, and on the way to see the brand new Stade de France for the first time. They were like me, yet in many ways so completely different; after all, none of them had started their football careers as a ten year old with Potter Street Rangers in the Harlow Recreational League in Essex. I don't mind admitting that at that moment I thought how far I'd come and – looking ahead to the summer – how far I wanted to go.

The stadium – when we finally got there through the Paris traffic – was breathtaking. The only disappointment was a bumpy, discoloured pitch that was blamed on a recently played rugby international. 'Ideal for us against Brazil' commented Craig Brown, beaming broadly and looking ahead to the match that would open France '98. He should be so lucky!

The dressing rooms were ultra-modern and very impressive, and I found myself imagining what it would be like to be in there with England on 12 July for the World Cup Final. I admit I visualized every detail in my mind – the players and staff getting ready, the warm-ups, the bell telling us it's time to go out. Then, the surge of adrenalin as we came out on to the pitch ... Another moment of pride was having my picture taken on the steps outside the stadium with the other coaches.

But the pitch wasn't all that concerned me. I'd been looking forward to the 'Workshop' (which was really just another name for a conference) but the priorities seemed wrong. Security, commercial considerations, tickets, pleasing the media and pre-match entertainment are all very well, but isn't the World Cup really about football? It didn't seem the number one subject at all.

Also, considering there were just three months to go until kick-off I thought they were asking for the coaches' input far too late in the day. Surely it would have made more sense to stage the conference at the time of the draw in December 1997 when all the coaches were last together, even if that did seem a generation ago.

As it was, there were two hours of discussions involving

just the coaches led by the Frenchman Gerard Houllier, who as a manager tried to buy me for Paris St Germain. To begin with I felt my age – here I was as the rookie coach. But not for long, since Gerard kept bringing me into the debate, seeking my views on things like warm-up times, and the idea of an electronic board to show the injury time remaining.

At least there were a few football issues up for discussion, namely the new ruling on the tackle from behind. If it was really going to be interpreted as strictly as they claimed, I was sure there would be masses of red cards in the early matches. In fact, I half-expected to see some nine-a-side games.

But at least England would have a chance to get to grips with the situation since we wouldn't be playing our first match until the tournament was five days old. I believed our players, people like Tony Adams and Martin Keown, could adapt. They would have to as they couldn't expect either the rules or the referees to change for them. It was up to the players and the coaches to adapt, and to help us we had decided to invite England's World Cup referee, Paul Durkin, to our training sessions before we left. (If he hadn't been available I might have asked David Elleray, even if he did give two penalties against my Chelsea team in the 1994 F.A. Cup Final!)

The other major footballing issue up for discussion was the coaches' request to have the squad number increased from twenty-two to twenty-three players to allow everyone to have a third goalkeeper for emergencies, as in Euro '96. Ludicrously, we didn't get our way. Instead we were told to make do with a spare named keeper on standby back home.

Just as ludicrous was the choice of our so-called 'liaison officer' whom the French organizers appointed to travel with us in the summer to help with any problems off the pitch. He was introduced to us at the workshop but within minutes of meeting him it became obvious he was quiet and impossible to talk to – in English! He had to go after we found ourselves sitting around the dinner table talking in pidgin French to help him understand. Politely and diplomatically, we had to say 'non, non, non' – and ask for a replacement. On reflection I think he was a football person who was much more interested in knowing our training schedules than anything else.

Overall though, those three days in Paris in March did give me a huge buzz as the World Cup countdown continued. OK, so I had the odd moan and groan, but as I kept saying to my staff, 'Imagine if we hadn't made it to France; if Christian Vieri's header in Rome had gone in; if we were staying at home?' Mind you, things were getting more difficult – on and off the pitch.

The defeat by Chile at Wembley was followed by a 1–1 draw in Berne against Switzerland on 25 March, after which I no longer had to worry about any euphoria and over-optimism! It was a really poor performance, which wasn't surprising considering that nine players from my original squad withdrew, making it quite impossible to work on the shape of the team in training.

It was doubly frustrating when several of those we lost played for their clubs just seventy-two hours after the international. I knew the press wanted me to be critical, but frankly, it's up to the managers and the players when they're with their clubs. I do think there's more inclination for clubs to play players who aren't totally fit, but I trusted the views of my medical people, so let's just say that some of the boys were unlikely to have been 100 per cent.

I had a bit of a laugh at those – like Richard Keys of Sky Television – who saw me on television during and after the match in Berne and thought I was showing the pressure. The truth was I had flu and felt pretty groggy. I'd had to miss the 'B' game the night before; I'd felt really hot and sweaty over my tea and toast that night and discovered I was running a temperature of 102 degrees. Maybe I should have blamed David Davies, who hadn't been well either, but it was more likely a sign that I was run down and needed a break. I stayed in my room throughout the day of the match until we left our hotel for the stadium. Doc Crane's paracetamol got me through it.

So when I appeared to end an after-match interview with Sky rather abruptly it had nothing to do with pressure. I'd already done one 'flash' interview immediately after the final whistle, which turned out to have been with Swiss TV. I was then confronted by both Sky and ITV, and after five questions – the 'flash' interview is supposed to be nothing more than a short sharp reaction to the game – I was determined to get back to the dressing room. I knew I would have to get used to these 'flash' interviews for the World Cup, but frankly they're the last thing I want at the end of a game. Surely coaches would give a better interview given time to gather their thoughts.

The incident underlined the huge demands of the media after matches, not least abroad. In Berne I faced interview after interview – television, radio, three separate press conferences – and still the questions kept coming. So was it surprising that in a deserted Berne airport lounge, at gone midnight after the Switzerland game, I said to the Sunday press: 'To be frank, I couldn't care two monkeys what you think'? It might have been said out of exasperation, but I meant it.

I needed to mean it when the story broke about me encouraging the England players to see a healer in our hotel: my long-time friend Eileen Drewery.

Let's get one thing clear: the timing of the story was deliberate. It was my decision to tell the media that Eileen had been visiting the team hotel in the build-up to our match with Portugal in April. I also told them that three quarters of our players had been to see her in recent months. There was actually nothing very new in the revelations because it was already common knowledge that players like Gazza and Paul Merson had visited Eileen, and that I believed in her.

Eileen heals through spiritual cleansing. I've relied on her for spiritual guidance for a long time, but even I don't totally understand the special gifts she possesses. Her techniques include the laying of her hands on the head and other special centres of the body.

I first met Eileen Drewery when I was eighteen and had just got into the Spurs first team. I'd started going out with her daughter Michelle and went round to her house one day for coffee. I didn't know Eileen was a healer then, but I happened to be out of the game with a torn hamstring at the time. As I was leaving she turned round to me and asked me what my injury was. I told her I'd torn a hamstring playing football. She didn't know that I was a professional.

When she told me she was going to do some absent prayer, I looked at her really strangely. I thought, 'What's this all about?' It's quite a natural reaction; I understand why people react like that when I talk about her now. But she told me to see if the injury was any better in the morning – and it was. It was incredible. There was no more pain. The Spurs physio Mike Varney had told me I'd be out for six to seven weeks ... but I trained two days later and played on the third day. The experience had a profound effect on me. I got to know her during the six months that I went out with Michelle, but over the next ten years I continued to see Eileen off and on for different injury problems. Often, her healing had a direct effect on the injury. At other times, like when I had an Achilles heel problem in 1984, she told me that I would have to have an operation but that the healing would help speed up my recovery after the operation.

About two years later, just before I went to the World Cup in Mexico, I had a slight knee problem: my patella tendon was inflamed and it wouldn't clear up. Normally, a couple of sessions with Eileen would have put it right but seven weeks later I was still visiting her. We couldn't work out why. However, there was a big change going on in my life at that time: I was asking questions, both of myself and of Eileen, about the meaning of life. I suppose I was beginning to realize that there was more to my life. She explained that much of the gift she had was down to God, that she was just a channel. It was then that I really started to think along spiritual lines. My life started to change and really blossom in the sense that I started seeing it from a completely different – and much deeper – perspective. My knee started to get better immediately.

Often Eileen and I would talk for five or six hours. She would explain to me how healing works, and I would go off searching for my own answers. Over a period of time everything started falling into place. On the spiritual side my faith in God got stronger and stronger. Just before the World Cup in 1986 I visited Israel where I had an amazing feeling that I was on the right track. I'd never felt that before.

My dad was cured of his arthritis of the back after just one session with Eileen. Now he plays golf every day and he's never had a problem with it since. That's just one incident. There are many, many more. But as far as football is concerned I started using her gift at Swindon although she had had a few sessions with my team mates when I was at Spurs. I thought, 'I've seen so many people helped by her that I'd be silly not to encourage some of the players to see her.' She had a particularly profound effect on a lad called Richard Green. When I took over I was told his career was finished. He had a back problem and had been to every surgeon and every doctor available. They all said he'd never play football again. I offered to introduce him to Eileen. I just asked him to keep an open mind – if you are sceptical it definitely blocks the healing process. He went to see her and when he came back he got into the reserve side and then in the first team before moving on to Gillingham. Ten years later he's still playing. I know that if he hadn't seen her, there's no way on this earth that he'd have been playing football today. There are many others like him; some have had career-threatening injuries, others have had smaller problems, but Eileen has helped all of them.

I've never forced anyone to go and see her. It's always down to them. But it's been intriguing sometimes to see hardened professional footballers come away from visiting Eileen having had a profound experience. Of course some of them wonder what it was all about and just get on with their lives. They are the ones who have missed out. You have to take what she says on board and think about it, and try and understand how the healing works and how it can change your life as it has for some but not for others.

I waited until my second get-together as England coach, when several of the players were carrying injuries, before asking if anyone wanted to see her. I told them about my experiences, about how she'd been a help to me since I was about eighteen years old. I asked them to open their minds to the idea and many of them did, including Les Ferdinand, Ian Wright, Sol Campbell and Darren Anderton.

Over an eighteen-month period the players would go and see Eileen, predominantly for physical problems at the beginning, but increasingly for mental support. It's very complicated but there are certain centres in the body that can be opened up and if they are they can have a damaging effect on the mind. It is difficult to explain and really it is Eileen's story to tell. Many of the players started going back to her between England get-togethers. I think they found it interesting and, to be frank, they saw the effect it had. They saw how good they felt and they saw their injuries clearing up.

Darren Anderton was a case in point. I'd been trying to get Darren to see Eileen for a year before he eventually did. I had spoken to his then manager at Spurs, Gerry Francis, who had seen one of his QPR players, Danny Maddix, make a spectac-ular recovery from a career-threatening injury thanks to Eileen's healing. I asked Gerry to help Darren because the boy had been out for a year and we were missing out as much as he was. A couple of operations later Darren started seeing Eileen. The healing was very powerful. I saw a change in him immediately. He was so positive in his approach. He went back to see her once a week, every week, for the next seven months and it's refreshing to see somebody come through all that he has had to contend with so successfully.

The cynics will say that the players go to see her just to please me. If that was true then why have players been to see her between England matches? Those up north used to fly down and see her, while I've known players who have flown back from abroad to see her. It was nothing to do with trying to impress me; it was to do with getting their careers back on track.

People would be astonished at the amount of players she's seen (although most of the people she sees are not foot-ballers; I've sent people I've known from all walks of life to see her). The bottom line is that footballers want to be fit, fit enough to play for their clubs and their country.

One particular day Paul Merson came to me at Burnham Beeches and I could see he was really negative just by look-ing in his eyes. He was in a dark tunnel, thinking all sorts of negative things about his family situation and his football. We were a bit worried about him. I think he was almost tempted to go back down the rocky road. I asked him if he wanted to go and see Eileen (he'd seen her in the past and had great results). He went that afternoon – and I have never seen anyone change so much. When he came back he was a different guy. He had the sparkle back in his eyes. He was positive, upbeat. He was reformed, if you like. It was an amazing transformation.

I know what she does but she will explain it herself in her

own book. Her healing has had an affect on many different people – she was using her wonderful gift when I first met her when I was eighteen. She is so down to earth and uncomplicated. When she explains how she uses God's power through love she makes it all sound so simple. Look at Jesus. You didn't find him in the churches. He actually challenged the churches of his day. His disciples were fishermen. He was a normal run-of-the-mill sort of guy who had a genuine gift, just as Eileen has got. God works through such people. Understanding how they work is an individual thing, a search within yourself for positive solutions and positive answers. Most people look for answers outside themselves, but the answers are on the inside. It doesn't matter if you are a pub landlord, a politician, or even royalty. We are all equal in God's eyes.

I've never once forced any of the players to see her. It's entirely up to them (although I wanted everyone to pay her a visit before we went to France because I thought they would all benefit). But I knew that as soon as she worked more closely with the squad in the team hotel the story would soon come out in a sensational way, and that it would be destructive if it happened in the days leading up to our departure for France. So I decided to make it public when it suited me.

Later I discovered some journalists had heard what was happening, and were saving their stories up. So if you like, what I did pre-empted the story I knew would come out and got it well and truly out of the way before the World Cup.

To begin with, the reaction was precisely as I'd expected. There were plenty of references to barmy armies, voodoo managers and mumbo jumbo. One television reporter went so far as to ask me to my face if I was a crank. Others were more open-minded; sceptical maybe, but not blatantly hostile.

The story certainly made the headlines and predictably, Eileen got the full media treatment: journalists and photographers camping out on her doorstep and following her for days.

Her daughter and her family got the same. Money was offered – in one case £50,000 to the former husband of one of Eileen's close relatives – for negative stories about her that in turn would discredit me and more importantly, God, who's gift Eileen has. I knew she could handle it though, and she did.

What I hadn't bargained for was the stories continuing for so long after my announcement, or the ferocity of the criticism from some ex-professionals like Alan Mullery and Martin Peters, not to mention the continuing interventions of Uri Geller.

The F.A. had got used to Geller's attempts to 'help' during Euro '96, when he'd offered his services to Terry Venables. Now – by strange coincidence at the same time as he was publishing a book – very publicly he offered to 'help' me. To begin with I ignored some of his claims. I wish I hadn't.

It's true that I met him, along with Eileen, her husband Phil and the former Chelsea player Paul Elliott, almost four years ago. But when the *News of the World* published Geller's inaccurate version of what happened at that meeting, I decided enough was enough, and called in the lawyers. Enough said.

Meanwhile, I'd gone ahead with my plan to have a break right at the beginning of April and flew to Barbados for a week with Vanessa Shean, whom I've been going out with since January. We weren't hiding. In fact, I'd told my wife Anne in advance that I was going, and Vanessa's husband, whom she's separated from, knew as well.

So – very quickly – did the press. The editor of one national newspaper even rang The F.A. to ask where I was going hours after I flew out to the Caribbean, so I can't say I was surprised to see pictures of Vanessa and me on the beach and in the sea in a Sunday newspaper. I just wonder if those concerned gave any thought to the reactions of our children? And before anybody tells me I should have thought about that before leaving home, perhaps they might also ask themselves what public interest is remotely served by the publication of such pictures.

The holiday did me good, but it was still a boost to get back with the players before the Portugal match at Wembley. We deliberately called up thirty-four, and I made it clear at the squad announcement that it was crunch time. I wanted them all there and they all came, even the wretchedly unlucky Jamie Redknapp, who suffered another leg injury against Coventry on Sunday 19 April, the day the squad gathered. I feel really sorry for Jamie.

The Manchester United contingent seemed in reasonable spirits, despite the fact that in recent weeks Monaco had ended their Champions' League dream and Arsenal had overtaken them in the Premiership. It was my job to lift the United boys mentally, which I did. I talked to them individually, reminded them that, whatever the disappointments of the season, they had the World Cup to look forward to. They responded really well in training. But I was still concerned that if people kept telling players like David Beckham, Teddy Sheringham and the Neville brothers that they looked tired, they would start to believe it. Brazilian players like Ronaldo and Roberto Carlos have been playing solidly for almost two years and no-one says they're tired. In fact, they're still the World Cup favourites, despite losing at home to Argentina.

The Arsenal players didn't need any lifting. Not surprisingly, David Seaman – who hadn't played for England since Rome – and Tony Adams, were a revelation. Tony's fitness still concerned me, but I could see that the good habits instilled in him by Arsène Wenger had made a big impact, likewise with Ray Parlour. What they eat, what they drink, when they eat and when they drink is all carefully controlled. I intended to do the same with my players in the summer.

He might not thank me for saying it, but Arsène will certainly be an international manager himself one day, I'm sure of that. He's made for the job: he is so knowledgeable, so organized and so loyal to his players. I'm thrilled for him that he's achieved so much so soon at Arsenal.

Meanwhile, it was a relief to see Gazza's future being sorted out with his move to Middlesbrough. At least it gave him clear targets: promotion with Boro and a World Cup place. I think the possibility of a move to America had been on his mind for too long – he was even talking about it before Le Tournoi – and although he was not seeing Eileen as much as I would have liked, at least Bryan Robson seemed to have sorted him out. His fitness still wasn't right, though. He'd definitely lost the definition in his legs and wasn't fit enough to play against Portugal, which was why I released him early.

Against Chile a few players – no names – had failed on the night, while against Switzerland – with all our injuries – we had been unable learn much of value. We were now less than two months from the start of our World Cup campaign. Well, I suspect it was only me who wouldn't have minded too much if we had lost to Portugal. The whole country seemed desperate for a good result.

Portugal should have made it to France as far as I was concerned. They were certainly talented enough. In their qualifying group they'd given Germany a real fright and if they hadn't had a man ridiculously sent off they might have won the game. So I knew I'd need most of my big guns for this one and thankfully, I got them. My spine – Seaman, Adams, Ince and Shearer – was in place for a game I'd always earmarked as a World Cup rehearsal, and I was delighted with the result, especially our second-half performance. When Alan Shearer scored that wonderful third goal I got a tingle down my spine. It was a lovely feeling.

We'd had to adjust in defence because they'd surprised us by playing three up front. People have this perception of me as a rigid three-at-the-back man but it's not entirely true. That's the way I like to play when we're in possession because it gives us a better shape, with three in midfield and the wing-backs pushing forward. But when we're defending we often revert to four at the back, and that's what we were looking to work on in the Portugal game. We needed Graeme Le Saux to push forward more.

But I couldn't get that message across to the players during the first half. That can be a very frustrating aspect of coaching. I came down from the stands and was screaming out for the chance to sort things out during a decent break in play, but it never happened. Luckily we coped OK and even went ahead, but at half-time we changed things around and within a few minutes of the second half I could see the shape of the game changing before my eyes. Some of our movement was first class, and it was certainly how we would have to play in France in some of our games.

In the end the game was won 3–0 but we could have managed more goals and certainly should have had five. I'll never know why Michael Owen wasn't allowed to go on when he was one-on-one with the goalkeeper (the referee failed to play the advantage rule) or why Tony Adams had a characteristic headed goal disallowed. It was hardly surprising that John Gorman and Ray Clemence on the bench got really wound up with the fourth official. Some of their language was what you might call typically 'benchlife'! He took offence and in protest all the Spanish officials boycotted the after-match meal in the Wembley Banqueting Hall.

Surprisingly the story never came out, but it didn't stop us winding John up afterwards that he might be banned from the World Cup. It taught us a lesson. In June, only the coach would be allowed to stand up, so we all had to get used to that.

A good night was somewhat spoiled on the way out of Wembley with the news that Paul Ince had been punched by a so-called supporter at the bottom of the steps leading from the stadium. Luckily he wasn't badly hurt, but it was a shocking experience. His wife, who saw what happened, was very upset. I spoke to Incey later on the mobile phone as he headed back to Liverpool. I wanted him to press a complaint against the man who was arrested, but Paul was worried that the distraction of a court case might interfere with his World Cup preparations, and decided against taking the matter further.

At least Wembley promised an investigation into its security arrangements immediately. I know there's no such thing as 100 per cent security, but too often, players and managers entering and leaving stadiums at home and abroad have to worry about this kind of thing. Personally I'd support harsh punishments for those who step out of line.

Leaving Wembley myself that night, I felt as content as I could about our progress. What I didn't tell the media during the usual succession of news conferences was that I knew my chosen twenty-two for France, fitness and form permitting. Having said that – not to mention the fact that there was no way I intended playing my strongest side and giving the opposition a head start – I would be giving everyone a run-out over the course of our remaining fixtures. But I was going to enjoy all the pundits predicting the squad during the next few weeks. It wasn't going to make a blind bit of difference to me!

On the pitch I was content with our progress towards France. But off it, there was a different story altogether. Not that I had any idea of the drama that was about to unfold when – along with John Gorman, David Davies, Brian Scott and our international administration assistant Michelle Farrer – I paid my last pre-tournament visit to the Hotel Du Golf International near La Baule in Brittany, which was to be our base throughout the Finals.

It had been our lucky home at Le Tournoi, and I knew then that it suited us perfectly. It's very secluded yet there's plenty of space and the rooms are large. A golf course runs alongside it and there's a pool as well as enough room for us to bring in all the medical and recreation facilities we might need. Even the restaurant, which was too small last year, had been extended. I could say no more than that I felt I was coming home, and I was sure most of the players would feel the same when they arrived in June.

But this was Wednesday 29 April, the real thing still two months away, and after a late dinner with the hotel manager Yannik Paturel, we headed for our beds. I was woken the next morning at 6.30 a.m. by a lawnmower, which was annoying but useful. I made a mental note to tell the golf course that our players would not be so tolerant just hours after returning late from their World Cup exertions.

I dropped off to sleep again, but it wasn't long before Sky News woke me with something I didn't want to hear. Alan Shearer, my captain, was front-page news as well as back. Had he deliberately kicked Leicester's Neil Lennon in the face at Filbert Street? My first impression was that I'd seen loads of similar incidents. In slow motion, however, it looked ten times worse.

Knowing Alan, though, it was sure to have been an accident. Perhaps he had reacted, but he had controlled himself. I was never to change my mind. If England's No. 9 had really intended to follow through I dread to think what the consequences would have been for Neil Lennon, and Alan himself.

I expected the controversy to last twenty-four hours. How wrong I was. What followed in the media over the next few days showed exactly what being Alan Shearer, and captain of England, really means. Everybody had a point of view, and the fact that I saw at least three far worse incidents in the next three games I watched counted for nothing.

The F.A. was widely criticized for not making its disciplinary intentions clear very quickly, but the reasons for that are straightforward. The people who were to play a major part in the proceedings, in particular Chief Executive Graham Kelly, were out of the country. By the time he returned it was the Bank Holiday, which delayed matters still further.

I was certainly not involved in the discussions that followed, despite reports suggesting otherwise. Graham Kelly decided there was a case to answer and while I accepted that, I was far from happy. I was seriously concerned that we could lose Alan for the World Cup campaign. I'd talked to him. I knew how upset he was. I knew his reaction to being charged by The F.A. would be unpredictable. I even thought that Alan Shearer might walk out of the England team for France.

Alan believed that by charging him, The F.A. doubted his assurance that what had happened was an accident. He believed they were questioning his honesty. I talked to him several times on the phone and asked him to think very carefully before he reacted. I didn't want other people's decisions and actions to deprive him of his World Cup dream. I pleaded with him: 'Make sure that whatever you do you'll never regret it. What if England don't qualify in 2002?'

I don't know how close Alan came to staying at home. Perhaps even he doesn't know. I believe it was a serious possibility, and who knows what the consequences of that might have been. I, for one, can't be sure how I would have reacted either if Alan had quit. OK, so Graham Kelly was doing what he felt was right and necessary, but it was a crisis for me, a major headache. I felt that I was the man in the middle.

Eventually, a twenty-four-hour delay in announcing F.A. action gave everyone time to reflect. It was Alan's request – nothing to do with me – that the case was heard quickly, and, as I'd always expected, an F.A. disciplinary commission effectively cleared my captain. Nobody expected or wanted Alan to get special treatment, although from the media at least, he did. He had reason to complain that the campaign against him in the media was based on who he was and not what he did.

Back at La Baule, meanwhile, we were facing another crisis. The pitch at our L'Escoublac training ground was very, very disappointing: patchy, bumpy and worn in places. It was so poor that we'd have been in big trouble had we not had six weeks to sort it out. A lack of the right equipment and quality advice meant that it was in far worse condition than when we'd seen it a year ago. We decided that the only solution was to call Wembley! The ground staff there would know exactly what was needed.

Frankly, I don't think the locals were very pleased. I got the vibes to suggest as much, despite my limited French. But for us it was an emergency; having to search for a couple of decent alternative training grounds was not what we wanted so close to the tournament. Fortunately, having driven around for hours in the rain – it always seemed to be raining when we were in La Baule – we found two exceptionally good sites just over twenty minutes away. I wondered why the organizers hadn't shown them to us in the first place, eighteen months previously, before Le Tournoi.

During those forty-eight hours in La Baule we met the local mayor. A glass of champagne was downed and toasts and presents exchanged. David Davies made a very long speech in French! I was more concerned about that L'Escoublac pitch. I suppose you could say I gave the mayor a diplomatic bollocking. Certainly it produced results.

We had liked L'Escoublac as a training ground from the day we'd seen it in the snow in January 1997. It's nice and secure, ideal for a World Cup campaign. But the French hadn't as yet fulfilled their promises. We hoped they would.

In the same week we were in La Baule, other F.A. groups were visiting Marseilles, Toulouse and Lens, our three certain venues in France. It's worth doing your bit to show you appreciate your hosts. In La Baule I handed out badges and pennants in a local school to several hundred children. In front of French TV cameras and photographers I picked up a little girl and hugged her. She clung on and wouldn't let go. Eventually she was clinging to a very tender and rather personal part of my body. Luckily, the journalists present didn't notice. I suspected their English counterparts might have done so – and written about it!

Despite Alan's problems and the setback over the pitch, our preparations were generally going very well. Several things would be markedly different from England set-ups in the past; one of which was that we would travel in our own plane, separately from the media, which is as much to do with practicalities as privacy. Things are very different now from the days when twelve journalists travelled with the England team; these days the media outnumber players and staff considerably – we took 107 journalists to Rome – and we just cannot afford delays at airports waiting for countless journalists to file their reports. It just can't be part of our planning.

Roger Narbett, our chef, was happier too. He would have to hire a new portable kitchen to back up the hotel's facilities, but for the first time at a World Cup the diet of the England team would be spot on.

Obviously, diet alone doesn't make the difference between winning and losing, but it can certainly improve performance, prevent injury and prolong careers, so it's vital to get it right. In many cases it means changing the habits of a lifetime; in my playing days it was fried food and Coca-Cola the day before a game with steaks all round on match day. Now we go in for lots of pasta and rice, boiled chicken and far less fat.

Gone are the days, too, when each player got his own favourite pre-match meal. Now everyone eats the same, although there's obviously some choice so that any vegetarians – like me – don't miss out: cold meats, tuna, hot dishes like cottage pie, but also lots of vegetables and pasta and a good range of puddings such as ice cream and fruit salad, or crumble. Close to a match day the ice cream and crumble will disappear, as will any chips, which rarely make an appearance these days. The Doc finds that hard to accept. He loves chips, and was very upset when they started playing a less prominent role! I imagine the players miss the odd burger and curry more. But they have to make some sacrifices and I think they understand that a lot of effort goes into determining the ideal diet. I do work closely with the chef on what's available each day.

We've also gone to some lengths to avoid cliques among the players and when we are in France we will encourage them to mingle during meal times by replacing small round tables with larger ones. I really believe that ideas like these are important to fostering a good team spirit, and everyone is generally very receptive.

Gary Lewin's also been giving the players food and vitamin supplements every day on the advice of Dr Jan Rougier, who I was fortunate to get to know at Monaco. He's what you might call a doctor of the body who's worked with winners right across the board – AC Milan, Monaco, and in the 1997–8 season, Arsenal. He's French and a friend of Arsène Wenger but he agreed to work with England during the World Cup.

I certainly felt a totally different player when I was at Monaco thanks to his advice, and I really believed his input would give us that extra 20 per cent in France. Each player has been screened and prescribed specific vitamin and mineral supplements on the basis of his recommendations. They were also given creatine which would kick in just before the tournament began. He advised them on everything: from what they should eat and when they should eat it to how to chew their food and take their drinks. For instance, there are still some clubs in England which give the players chocolate bars in the dressing room before a game, yet sugar is the last thing a player should have. It'll boost his energy levels but only for a limited period in a game. The principle is similar to looking after a car engine: if it's in great working order, and it's got a good driver, then it's going to be a winner.

England's preparation in the past was never this thorough. We had iron pills during the 1986 World Cup in Mexico, and drank lots of extra water. But that was about it. The Germans and Italians, on the other hand, have recognized the importance of diet over many years, and reaped the benefits. Thanks to the input of people like Dr Rougier, I can honestly say, hand on heart, that this was the best prepared England team ever.

When we're in France we will have to give chef Roger Narbett a night or two off so during our pre-tournament visit we looked at three different restaurants around La Baule. One in particular, on the seafront, looked ideal. We found it by coincidence in the same week the *Sunday Times* named La Baule as having one of the most beautiful beaches in the world. Pity we wouldn't have much time to enjoy it.

While there would be time to play some golf at the hotel, I was well aware of the dangers of boredom, even during the World Cup. Over the years I've learnt a simple way of counteracting dull moments: you just have to remind yourself of what you're doing, why you're doing it, and the millions of people you're doing it for. I used to remind myself about my childhood, about my roots, and about the heroes of the 1966 World Cup. I would tell myself, 'Just get on with it.' And it always worked.

That approach doesn't work for everyone, though, so we planned to allocate rooms for reading (for the likes of Tony Adams and Graeme Le Saux), rooms for television and videos, and even a 'mini arcade' with pool tables, table tennis, darts and video games, which should keep the Manchester United and Liverpool contingents amused.

The players would also be able to use our techno-gym which is geared towards individuals' fitness and rehabilitation and which our physio Alan Smith helped set up. It would be housed in one of the big villas in the hotel grounds. Our

medical centre, where the physios and masseurs would oper-
ate, would be in another of the villas, while our kit man Martin
Grogan would have his own villa, too. The coaches were to
meet in a separate building with its own video facilities.

We also pinpointed a meeting room. I had the sofas
removed – ordinary chairs are more difficult to doze off in –
and thankfully they've installed air conditioning since last
summer. True, my meetings don't last long (little more than
three minutes back in Rome, remember); my style is very different to that of my old Spurs boss Keith Burkinshaw and
Bobby Robson, who was England coach in my day. They
could hold a meeting and a half; it could last an hour or more.
But for me, meetings are all about topping up the bulk of the
work, which should have been done on the training ground.

One thing is certain: the players won't have any
newspapers to distract them. I decided there would be no
English papers – or at least the tabloids – delivered every day
during the World Cup. The risk of negative stories affecting
the players is too great. Of course they may hear about them
from home, or on the television. But they won't have to look
at often painful personal stories staring out at them in their
rooms or hear the other players chatting about them in the
restaurant. Nor will I or the coaches. In the past some players have been known to sneak into David Davies' room for a
quick read, but we would be doing our level best to keep
them out!

I can't expect to stop the media saying what they like
about football matters, nor do I want to. But I decided to do
what I could to persuade them that personal stories about the
players and staff of the shock-horror variety – we all know
what I mean – could be really harmful to our chances if they
were to appear during the tournament.

I told the editors and sports editors exactly how disruptive and damaging such stories could be when we met at a
specially arranged golf day at Stoke Poges in early May. I told

them that I feared these stories could tip the balance against us. I was speaking from experience; after all, I was there in Spain in 1982, and again in Mexico in 1986, when stories about the staff and players' private lives kept popping up. Who could forget the diabolical treatment Bobby Robson got in the build-up to Italia '90?

We discussed this appeal at The F.A. at length before I made it. The risk was that the press would react by going public and claiming that paranoia had set in. But I think the editors were intrigued. Some had apparently never thought seriously about the impact of such stories on young players. Inevitably, somebody asked what I'd do if they ignored my appeal. I told them I'd go public and name the paper that had damaged our chances. I meant it. I don't really think I was asking for too much, although time will tell.

Of course, it helped getting them on to the golf course. Everyone was more relaxed. I play off sixteen and think I'm quite a good golfer, but my playing days very nearly ended there and then thanks to a mishit drive by Rob Shepherd, sports editor of the *Express* and one of the worst golfers I've ever seen. He nearly killed me when he crashed his drive into the buggy I'd been sitting in seconds earlier.

The object of all this was obvious: we were determined to get the preparation right, to think of every detail to give ourselves the best possible chance in France. The recruitment of Tina Westfallen as welfare officer to the squad was another aspect of that. Tina took charge of the sort of things I know worry players during a World Cup: looking after families while they are away; arranging any necessary hospital appointments for wives and children; making family travel arrangements on match days; and what about birthdays? They may sound trivial, but little things like that can become time-consuming distractions in the minds of players preparing for the biggest sporting event on earth.

CHAPTER 4

WHO'S IN, WHO'S OUT

MAY 1998

Time was running out. By 1 June, my twenty-two names of those who would make history – the first England squad to win the World Cup abroad (or so I hoped) – would be named. As I've already said, injuries and fitness permitting, I knew the squad I would like; I'd known it for several weeks. But Gazza and Wrighty were definitely behind on their match fitness and really hadn't made the progress I'd hoped for. I was also concerned about Darren Anderton, Les Ferdinand, Jamie Redknapp and Tim Flowers.

So on 12 May at a press conference at Lancaster Gate I announced a squad of thirty for the friendly with Saudi Arabia plus a tournament – two matches, against Morocco and Belgium – in Casablanca. It was no surprise that all the media really wanted to talk about was not who was still in the squad, but who was already out of it.

So no Matthew Le Tissier. I'm reluctant to say it's the end of the international road for anyone, but to be honest he'd had a poor season by his standards. True, he scored a hat-trick for the 'B' team against a not very good Russian side at Loftus Road. But I think he knows just how much more we feel he should be contributing over ninety minutes. He's got talent in abundance but we need more from him physically and mentally if he's to reach the top. I'd have loved to have seen him playing for a Manchester United or a Tottenham or a Chelsea – clubs where the demands of the crowd are much higher week in, week out.

England has probably seen Stuart Pearce for the last time despite his international experience, which I know we're short of. But I'd noticed some chinks in his game defensively, and he'd taken time to recover from injuries, time that wouldn't be available in France. It was a difficult decision to leave him out, but one which Stuart – as a former manager himself – understood. I certainly don't regret persuading him back on to the international scene. It was never a case of, 'Do me a favour and see me through the qualifying games.' At the time I thought he could go all the way to France. But I can say no more than that he's been a great ambassador for his country. When I finally got through to him, he took the news magnificently.

No Andy Cole, either, which is hard on him because he's been unlucky. I wanted Andy to start against Chile, but he declared himself unfit on the morning of the game so never got to take his chance. I've gone on record as saying that Andy's problem is that he still needs three or four opportunities in front of goal before he takes one, and you don't get that many at international level. Wrighty, meanwhile, has proved he can do it for me, and I still hope that his enforced break through injury was a blessing in disguise.

Our news conference that sunny May day was almost over when somebody – I think it was John Dillon, most recently of the *Mirror* – mentioned Gazza. Was I concerned about him smoking?

I wasn't surprised: twenty-four hours earlier, another newspaper had tried to make it an issue. But quite frankly, some foreign coaches would have thought it farcical that I was being questioned about players smoking, since quite a few do. Most of my team-mates at Monaco smoked more than they drank. I don't like smoking myself, but I honestly felt that at this stage it might be detrimental to Gazza for him to stop suddenly.

Well, Gazza's smoking didn't become a big issue, but within days his other habits did. Again. And inevitably, since there were always photographers hanging around him, there he was on the front page of a tabloid newspaper being 'helped' out of a restaurant after a night with his high-profile friends; then munching a kebab in the early hours of the morning in Soho. In between times I had reliable people informing me he was still having lunch late in the afternoon. Some of those around me started to suspect for the first time that Gazza wasn't a certainty for France.

Once we got to Burnham Beeches to prepare for the Saudi game, I got Gazza into my room and told him in no uncertain terms that enough was enough. He had to get his mind and body focused. He had ended the season barely half-fit and was still getting injured because he was in such poor physical shape. He should have been trying harder.

I wasn't telling him anything new. I'd sat him down before the Portugal game in April, and before we played Chile in February. This time Paul Gascoigne left my room having been told exactly where he stood. There were no grey areas. For starters I'd told him he couldn't have any more alcohol unless I said so. I hoped the message would sink in, because I still thought we could train him, play him – and get him 100 per cent fit.

Meanwhile, it was soon over for Jamie Redknapp. He was already doubtful after the knee injury he picked up late in the season, but I wanted to see if he could come through a week of training with us. He couldn't.

He started brightly enough, but I needed to know for sure forty-eight hours before the Saudi game. I was down the other end of the training pitch at Bisham when I could see his stride pattern had changed. That night he was honest enough to go to my physios and tell them he wasn't right, that he wouldn't do himself justice in France. When I saw Jamie I simply told him that he was young enough to have a future. He has to be mentally strong enough to believe his luck will change. He's the sort of person you want to achieve something. He's a diamond lad.

Bang went my idea of playing Jamie in the sweeper's role then, although it was a long shot since the fact that Jamie doesn't play sweeper for Liverpool would have counted against him. Young Rio Ferdinand looks as if he has the potential to play there in the future, if he keeps progressing. But it's too soon to be sure.

Those players who were involved in Euro '96 were reacquainted with the dentist's chair early on that week, only this time for all the right reasons. I'd had a painful abscess while we were in Colorado just before the 1986 World Cup Finals in Mexico and it took two visits to a dentist out there to put it right. If the problem had arisen mid-World Cup I'd have been in deep trouble, and would have missed key games. So I'd learned my lesson, and to make sure we wouldn't get caught out by unnecessary problems in France we sent the entire squad to be checked over by a dentist friend of Ray Clemence's near Burnham Beeches. One or two, in particular David Beckham, needed extra treatment, but there was nothing more serious than that.

The Saudi game itself, on a Saturday afternoon at Wembley, gave me some satisfaction, even if I understood the media and fans getting frustrated; they will always be result-orientated. Since it was a friendly the edge to the game wasn't there. But a goalless draw had its advantages. To be sure, we were no longer going to France as World Cup favourites if the reaction of the press and public was to be believed.

Not only that, but I saw a lot of good movement against the Saudis which, if we'd scored early on, I'm sure would have led to several goals. Sometimes you play poorly yet get away with a 1–0 win which is then described as a great performance. Other times you play really well and carve the other team open, yet because you only manage a 1–1 draw you get criticized.

As a coach you have to detach yourself from all that. Believe me, I'm very, very critical of our performances, but I also know when I see positive things, things that we've worked on in training, come off. I saw lots against the Saudis.

Another bonus for me was that Darren Anderton came through with flying colours. He would be fit, and, I thought, we would be OK, too. Anyway, they say we're better with our backs up against it.

In the dressing room after the Saudi game I witnessed a moment that showed just how together the squad is. Andy Hinchcliffe and Phil Neville were considered by many – including some of the players – as competing for one place. Yet Phil was big enough to say, 'Well played, Andy,' and being Phil, he meant it.

The fans had obviously been up for the game. Now that the domestic season was over, their enthusiasm for the World Cup had reached fever pitch. Many of them still expected an England win in France, and their show of national unity was like a volcano erupting.

But there's no way that football is more important than life and death. I've never believed that, whatever Bill Shankly said or meant. However, there's no denying that success for the England team means so much to so many people, which is why I was so disappointed by the reported comments of my former chairman, Ken Bates, who seemed to be saying that international friendlies are a waste of time. Only clubs really matter. He can't see further than the end of the Kings Road, and it's very sad. Typically, though, Ken won't lose any sleep over it.

The Monday after the Saudi game, the papers were full of Gary Neville's criticism of those England fans who ganged up on our Manchester United players at Wembley by chanting 'Stand up if you hate Man U.' The *Express* quoted Gary as saying 'You're an absolute disgrace,' and I couldn't have put it better myself. I was furious, too, at the way a group of fans booed Darren Anderton, and was pleased for Darren that he won them round.

There wasn't much time to dwell on the aftermath since the following day we flew to Spain and arrived at La Manga, our base for our final warm-up matches before the World Cup, against Morocco and Belgium in Casablanca. There were no press on the flight from Luton; there wouldn't be any during our World Cup campaign, either. It makes such a difference. Everyone seemed more relaxed and there was more room, too.

On the final day at La Manga I was to reveal my final twenty-two, and the names of the seven players (less Jamie Redknapp) who hadn't made it. The announcement was to be made on the terrace of the Hyatt Regency Hotel. For weeks we'd been secretly planning to get the unlucky ones home immediately, within hours of me telling them. We also knew that once the players knew who was in and who was not, the secret would quickly be out, so we considered springing a surprise by announcing the twenty-two on the Sunday night, twelve hours ahead of schedule and after the seven had reached England.

We got a police escort from Murcia Airport, which is when it really hit me that the World Cup was almost upon us. Clem, who played in Spain in the 1982 World Cup, thought exactly the same thing.

La Manga was looking at its best when we arrived; they'd

even put out English flags and banners for our benefit. The training ground was perfect – the Norwegians have developed it to train on during their long winters and the pitches and the surroundings are ideal – the golf courses looked smashing, too. The only thing they hadn't seen to was the wind, which was a bit strong! We'd taken over the East Wing of the hotel. There was plenty of space, some wonderful views, and Roger Narbett set a fantastic standard with the meals he prepared (even if the absence of corn flakes in favour of less heavy options like juice, toast, poached eggs and yoghurt on match days caused a few moans and groans from both players and staff at breakfast). The players all seemed to love La Manga. I found myself wishing I could pick it up and transport it to France.

John Gorman took my place to talk to the media on that first night. I wasn't going to make myself available every day in France and wanted people to get used to that fact. People might claim I'm shirking my responsibility but my role is to win the World Cup for England, not talk to the media every day. I'm aware that someone has to, but it doesn't always have to be me. John enjoys it anyway, although I'm sure he prefers to talk about football rather than having to suffer questions like: 'What's been the biggest disagreement you've had with Glenn?' and 'Do you support Eileen Drewery's involvement?' They were just aimed at tripping him up and making tomorrow's headlines.

The beautiful weather at La Manga meant that the players had ample time to soak up some sun under supervision from Doc Crane, who made sure no one stayed out longer than forty-five minutes. Players must have time to relax in their own ways and personally, I think that lying in the sun for up to forty-five minutes a day can revitalize the energies. No reading, listening to music or chatting – just concentration on the sun. It's a form of meditation that provides thinking time without distraction. And you don't have to do it all at once if you're worried about burning. Unbeknown to me, however, the Doc told all and sundry that the worst player for 'sneaking round the corner for extra sun' used to be Glenn Hoddle!

This new slant on sunbathing might not be what previous England regimes went in for, and despite what the *Daily Mail's* Jeff Powell writes (supposedly quoting Steve McManaman) joining up with England is nothing like 'being part of a religious cult'. It's the second time Powell has said this. Steve denies it and contacted his solicitor who was equally furious. They decided to put out a statement the next day. Steve says he's never met Jeff Powell, and doesn't want to. But if it wasn't Macca who talked to the *Daily Mail* back in March, I wonder who it was? Perhaps I actually know!

Fortunately Paul Ince was OK to play in our first match in the King Hassan II tournament, against the home nation, Morocco, who have a similar style to Tunisia. The English press were astonished Incey was playing after his ankle injury, but it was his decision to declare himself fit – there's no way I'd have taken a risk with him. After a quick lunch and a rest in one of Casablanca's hotels we arrived at the stadium with two hours still to go before kick-off to find around 80,000 people already inside. We had to walk along an open passageway to the dressing room, which turned out to be a very unpleasant experience since some fans chose to shower the players with water and spit.

The crowd were pretty hostile; there was even a banner in the crowd in English telling us, 'We have good hotels here too,' referring to my decision not to stay overnight in Morocco. But I had no regrets. We'd committed ourselves to La Manga a long time ago when a friendly away fixture against Portugal looked on the cards and we weren't about to change our plans to pacify the Moroccans. We had lunch in one of their hotels, anyway, which was fine. I know the French and the Belgians, who also played in the tournament and were staying in hotels outside Casablanca, were surprised by our travel arrangements, but if they had seen La Manga they would have known why we were so keen to get back there.

The pre-match formalities turned into a marathon. From the other side of the pitch we didn't really know to start with what was going on, but it transpired that the wrong national anthem was played. Our boys, led by Incey, Gazza and Wrighty, insisted on singing the right one before posing for a team picture. Good for them. It was a memorable moment.

There was more farce when we discovered that the Moroccans' idea of neutral officials included a neighbouring Tunisian referee plus two linesmen from ... Morocco! But the game itself will be remembered for two things: Michael Owen's stunning goal – he's the youngest player in history to score for England – and Ian Wright's hamstring injury, which was the reason Michael was on the pitch in the first place. It was in the same leg as the long-term problem he's had with his groin, and since it was a hamstring I feared the worst, though I didn't say so to the press.

As I expected, once we got in front the Moroccans started to applaud us and turn against their own team. But I was bitterly disappointed by our performance. At least we turned it around in the second half, and I was pleased that Gazza lasted the full ninety minutes on his birthday; he received a present from the hotel and a cake on the flight home.

I was also thrilled that young Michael Owen got off the mark before France. It would take the pressure off him. But my heart was in my mouth when he collided with the knee of the Moroccan keeper and was out cold for a minute. I saw Dion Dublin spin him over quickly and thought he'd swallowed his tongue, and although the medical boys were dealing with it, I don't mind admitting I just wanted to be there. I just felt that I wanted to go out there and do something positive so I put my hand on his body and said a quick prayer ... eventually he came round. His first words were: 'I don't want to come off, I won't come off.' The boy showed a lot of courage to get up and go on to score the winner.

During the Sky interview after the match they tried to get me to confirm that I'd be taking Michael to France, but I wouldn't take the bait. In my mind I'd always known he'd be in the squad, even before he played for England. I just needed confirmation that he could do it for his country. It came against Chile back in February when he was doing things that made me think, 'Hang on, if so-and-so was in that position would he have done that?' And the answer was; 'No, he wouldn't have had the pace.'

Even then, coming off the back of that game I was keen to see how he reacted – and bang, he went and scored a hat-trick for Liverpool. Some youngsters would think: 'Well I haven't got to run around any more,' but this boy just went and scored three. Fantastic. I spent ages watching him over the next few weeks after that. Often, when I went to see Liverpool play, I wasn't watching what went on at the other end of the pitch but watching Michael, his movement and his runs. I did the same with Rio. I needed to know if they were going to be good enough for the World Cup. With Michael there was never any doubt.

Decision day was approaching but there was one thing that had been settled for me. Wrighty was out of the World Cup. I could have wept for him. He was examined by both doctors and our two physios and his hamstring needed a minimum of two weeks, by which time the World Cup would have been underway. I'm surprised at how well he seems to have accepted it. Perhaps I was closer to tears than him. 'It wasn't to be,' is what he said. He was spot on. Despite spending so long recovering from a groin injury, in the end he was done by something else. He would have made the squad. The type of character he is, he's bound to be missed, just as Jamie (Redknapp) will be. I'll invite him to join us in France. After all, he's one of the main reasons we got there.

The day after Gazza's birthday, I could see he wasn't right. Just the sort of story I'd warned might surface had got him down. A picture of his wife Sheryl with a new 'friend' appeared in a newspaper that by early afternoon was floating around the hotel. It was another example of why we wouldn't be having the tabloids delivered to La Baule.

We were also worried about Andy Hinchcliffe, who'd been complaining about a thigh strain for several days. He was now saying it was getting better, but I had my doubts and so did the staff.

As decision day approached, I wasn't looking forward in any way to telling those I wasn't taking to France. I thought a lot about how best to handle it. I wanted to do it in the best and the fairest way possible. That was face to face. But leaving somebody out of the World Cup squad doesn't compare to telling a teenage apprentice he's not going to make it in football. That's what I had to do on several occasions in my early days at Swindon and it was far, far worse.

We had another birthday celebration at the end of May. David Davies was fifty, and La Manga came up with a special birthday cake presented to David by a stunning blonde who we'd smuggled into the hotel without the media noticing. She looked suspiciously like a member of my coaching staff in drag – or at least her legs did! The make-up was so good it even deceived some of the lads ... I can confirm or deny nothing. Terry Mancini, the ex-QPR and Arsenal player who helped organize our La Manga visit, had also arranged a surprise party for the staff and David in my room. There was vintage wine, plenty of good conversation, some long jokes from Doc Crane, and a piece of Lladro china for David as a birthday present. He was near to tears on several occasions. It was a lovely night.

Before we returned to Casablanca for our match with Belgium – and the chance to win the King Hassan II Trophy

– we had to say farewell to Wrighty, who flew home to London. He stayed away from breakfast, I think because he didn't want the sadness of saying goodbye. John Gorman noticed Ian had a tear or two while he was talking to him, but he took his disappointment very well. What we didn't – and couldn't – have known was that his flight from Alicante was cancelled because of an industrial dispute. He ended up spending the night in the Spanish resort before finally getting away.

On the way back to Morocco, we learned that the *Daily Mail*'s back-page 'exclusive' claimed that Jimmy Five Bellies, Gazza's friend, had been staying at the hotel we were using in the Moroccan capital, and spent Wednesday there with Gazza on his birthday. Total, utter nonsense. Would the *Mail* apologize? If any of us coaches were to make a mistake like that we'd be crucified. (The *Mail* did print a short apology saying they'd got it wrong, but ten days later and stuck away on an inside page.)

The atmosphere at the Belgium game on the Friday was the total opposite to when we'd played Morocco two days earlier. This time, the stadium was almost empty when we arrived, in contrast to the 80,000 patriotic Moroccans who had greeted us with such a racket in the first game. Their Mexican wave was the fastest I'd ever seen. At least we didn't have to suffer being spat at again.

There wasn't much atmosphere in the dressing room before the game, either. In fact, you could have heard a pin drop it was so quiet. In hindsight, perhaps it was because Gazza wasn't there. He was out in the middle of the pitch, talking on his mobile phone. Again.

To be honest, he hadn't had the best of starts to the day when he'd kept the team bus waiting before we left for Casablanca. I'd been worried about him the day before, too. He'd spent most of the afternoon on the phone to his wife when he was meant to be resting and it seemed to have affected him mentally. I had a bit of a heart to heart with him after that; my personal situation was, after all, difficult too. But my patience was starting to wear thin by the time he'd kept us waiting for several minutes on the bus because he was on the phone again.

I deplore players being late leaving for a game because at that stage you want them to be focused and on time, and you don't want to upset anyone's concentration. David Beckham had been late for the Morocco game but I'd overlooked that. Becks wasn't even a sub that day, and to be fair he was the only player not to have got an alarm call from the hotel reception. But with Gazza it was different.

I'd decided against making a scene on the bus simply because it was match day and I didn't want any disruption. But when I saw him in the middle of the pitch with the phone to his ear, I couldn't help myself. I thought, 'I'm going to make a scene here.' When I realized how many cameras were focused on him I sent Glenn Roeder to deal with him instead. Gazza got off the phone pretty sharpish after that and came into the dressing room to prepare for the game.

But at that moment I started to seriously doubt he could do a job for us in France. Physically, he wasn't 100 per cent; mentally, he was all over the place and he hadn't pulled up any trees in the games. So I sat there on the opposite side of the dressing room from him thinking, 'This is a big game for you son, a very big game.'

I don't think he realized just how big it was. I think he was complacent, never dreamt in a million years that his place was on the line. All I said to him beforehand was that I wanted to see him last seventy minutes plus.

Of course, that didn't happen, but the game was still of great value to me. I think a lot of people thought I'd play my strongest side against the Belgians as it was our last proper friendly match before France, but I'm not that naïve. I know people have criticized me – 'Hoddle's too secretive about his line-ups', they say. But the fact of the matter is that I'm secretive about the important things. If I know how the opposing team is going to line up two days before a game, then I've got two days to prepare for that. It's a major advantage. Remember that's why we threw a couple of googlies at the Italians in Rome. It was such an important game.

In fact, I purposely played 4-4-2 against Belgium, playing Nicky Butt alongside Gazza, and gave Paul Merson a run-out up front with Les Ferdinand. I wanted to have a look at a different shape. But frankly, I could see it wasn't working ten minutes into the game. We weren't keeping the ball and were hitting it too long, too early. We looked methodical. We lacked any shape.

I gave the players a rollicking at half-time, really got tucked into them. I've never been one to rant and rave and throw coffee cups around, but I used some strong words, stronger than I'd normally use. I told the players they weren't doing themselves any favours. They knew I wasn't happy.

In the second half we were a different team. I took both the Neville brothers off – Phil unfortunately hadn't been at his very best for England in recent times – and put on Rio Ferdinand, and sent Michael Owen up front alongside Les Ferdinand. Michael's pace immediately gave us more movement and we started to create chances. We really should have scored. We looked assured at the back, too.

The only negative thing to come out of the second half was that Gazza had to come off after five minutes. He had a dead leg and a cut on the head. And it was at that moment, after all I'd seen of him physically and mentally that day, that I knew deep down he'd probably run out of time. Of course, I had to be positive during the press conferences after the game and not give out any signals that I was thinking of leaving him out. But afterwards, at the airport, I just sat and thought, and it kept coming to me that I couldn't take Gazza to France.

Actually, I wasn't meant to be at the airport at all. I should have been on my way to Frankfurt to see Germany play a friendly against one of our first-round opponents in France, Colombia. But the Spanish air traffic controllers' strike worried me. Would I get stuck in Germany, unable to get back to tell the players who was going to France as planned on the Sunday night, something only I could do? It had taken Graham Kelly eight hours to get to Casablanca flying over Spain. I couldn't risk that happening to me.

In the end, John Gorman went to Frankfurt instead. It was a last-minute decision; John even had to wear my shoes and belt, and our travel manager Brian Scott's suit, because he hadn't brought one to Casablanca with him. Ironically, if I'd listened to my intuition I could have warned John to pack his suit after all. I'd woken up at La Manga on Friday morning with a hunch that I wouldn't be going to Germany. I couldn't explain it. But as it panned out – after all that went on in the game and the situation with Gazza – it was obvious that I wasn't meant to go. It was like a jigsaw falling into shape.

I couldn't get Gazza out of my mind the next day. I'd slept well – I always sleep well – but I couldn't rest mentally. The question kept going round and round in my head, 'Can you honestly say that Gazza is going to last seven games in France? Will he really be back to his very best?' And I kept coming back to the same answer. No.

But I had to switch off. I'd have driven myself mad other-wise. Like a lot of football people I relax on the golf course, so that afternoon I had a four-ball with Terry Mancini against Darren Anderton and Gary Neville. They were both bandits and I lost money, but it was still a terrific game! Terry and I saved the back nine on the last hole. It really cleared my mind.

That night, while the players were in the bar – I'd told them they deserved to have a few beers and enjoy themselves – we had a coaches' meeting: just Ray Clemence, Peter Taylor and myself, since John was still in Germany. We talked at length, about lots of different issues, but inevitably the discussion turned to Gazza. I told them I wasn't sure about him. Apparently, I wasn't the only one. The feeling was that the fact that it was Gazza was clouding the issue; had the doubts surrounded any other player, he wouldn't have been in the squad. No question about it.

In the end I phoned John Gorman in Germany and told him my thoughts. We decided I should sleep on it and phone him in the morning if I'd changed my mind. I was pretty certain I would not be picking up that phone.

By that time it was about 11 p.m., and before turning in for the night we decided to go down and join the players in the bar. They were all there, all the players. But Gazza stood out. Gazza was drunk. As I walked down those stairs and saw him there, I knew then that we couldn't take him to France. He wasn't out of order. Actually, he was having a good sing-song on the karaoke. Just about everyone had had a few beers, but no one had had as many as Gazza.

We were in that bar until the players left at about 1 a.m. Gazza had already left. He was ushered up to his room by David Seaman. I didn't speak to him. I ignored him. Whatever I had to say to him could wait.

We had planned the following day – decision day – down to the last detail. We knew we had to get what would now be six players who were to be left out away from the squad and from La Manga as soon as the news was out. I genuinely felt that the last place those players would want to be was with the rest of the squad – the lucky ones, so to speak.

We had also decided, earlier in the week, to publicly name the axed players on the Sunday night rather than on the Monday as planned. It was obvious that once the players themselves knew, the secret would not stay that way for long. In fact, considering the number of people who did know our plans beforehand – the people running the private aeroplane that flew the players back to Birmingham, some of the staff at La Manga and the airport staff – it was amazing that we managed to keep it quiet as long as we did.

I might have woken on that Sunday morning with a heavy heart, but I actually felt very bubbly. The sun was shining and the setting was perfect – I sat having breakfast looking over the golf courses towards the mountains in the background – and I knew that I had made the right decision. It wasn't that I was going to enjoy telling the six players they were missing out, but that I knew I had to do it. I felt as positive as I could.

By 10 a.m. our international administration secretary Michelle Farrer had put up a notice board with five-minute slots for each player to come to see me. The first appointment – David Seaman – was at 4.15 p.m. I had given Michelle a list of when I wanted to see the six unlucky players. They weren't going to be at the front and they couldn't be at the end because we had to get them out of the hotel to the airport by the time I had finished briefing the rest of the players. So they had to be among the first eleven players I saw.

Before all that, however, I had to get even on the golf course. Needless to say, I couldn't concentrate over the first nine holes but on the back nine ... well Terry Mancini and I gave Darren and Gary a hammering. It did me good anyway! The latter part of the afternoon, I knew, was going to be far less enjoyable.

The meetings took place in the wonderful Royal Suite that Brian Scott, our travel manager, had organized for me. It was a fantastic room, one of the best I've ever stayed in. Amongst other things it has a superb CD system which I'd noticed when we visited La Manga in the winter. I'd made a mental note to bring a selection of CDs with me and had Kenny G playing in the background because I felt that some of the players might be a bit nervous walking into a silent room. But I moved the complimentary bottle of wine and two glasses that had been in the middle of the table into the kitchen. Something told me that it might be a good idea.

The first unlucky player I saw was Ian Walker. We had a discussion about his form, which I felt had been a bit below par. He was just a bit rustier than the other keepers. He took on board what I had to say, which was that with the talent he's got there's a good chance he could end up as England's No. 1 if he stays injury-free. He was obviously disappointed, but I think he half-expected my decision. He seemed in a positive frame of mind when he left.

Phil Neville was a tough one. He was very, very upset. He couldn't talk. He just shook my hand and I felt very sorry for him. I had to explain that a year ago I'd been really pleased with him, but that since then he hadn't been hitting me in the eye when he played for England.

Dion Dublin was the hardest in many ways since he was so close to making it. If Ian Wright had been fit then I would have plumped for Dion's versatility rather than Les Ferdinand's pace. But Dion was also the easiest to tell because he took it like an adult. His reaction was first class. He told me he thought he'd done enough, but that he respected my decision.

I had a long chat with Nicky Butt. I told him that if I was a Premiership manager looking to buy a midfielder who would guarantee me thirty-eight games a season, he'd be top of my list. I meant it. But I just felt that at this level he wasn't quite ready. With a bit more experience he could become a mainstay in the England team.

Andy Hinchcliffe certainly had a good chance of making the final twenty-two, but in the end his thigh problem counted him out.

By this time it was 5.30 p.m. and we were running approximately twenty minutes late. The next name on the board was Paul Gascoigne.

I already knew that the next few minutes were going to be

stormy. I'd received a phone call from one of my staff just before David Seaman had come in, marking my card that Gazza was half cut again. At that moment I thought, 'He's made this very easy for me, very easy.' But it wasn't that easy after all.

There was a bang on the door. I knew it was Paul. He was more drunk than I thought he would be. I think he had bumped into Glenn Roeder and read his face. And he knew. That's when he stormed in. I sat him down and he muttered something like, 'I don't believe this.' I said, 'Well, you're not fit enough. It's nothing to do with anything else.' And he began to cry.

I had a strange sense of déjà vu at that moment. Two days before, on the night of the Morocco game, I'd dreamt that Gazza was sitting across the table from me crying his eyes out. At the time I didn't quite understand the significance of the dream. Suddenly, however, it all became clear.

Gazza got up and was saying, 'I don't believe this, gaffer, my career is finished.' But I knew he didn't mean it. He was drunk. I thought about trying to talk to him but knew I couldn't, not while he was in this state. He would never take it in. Suddenly he stopped, moved closer to me and shook my hand. 'I'm going to wish you all the best,' he said.

I stood up too and squeezed his shoulder. I said, 'Look, we've just run out of time with you.' I wanted to go into the situation, explain how he could have helped himself, but he turned to go – then suddenly he flew into a total rage and kicked the chair. It was a full-blooded volley and I was concerned because he had bare feet. He could have broken his foot, he kicked it so hard. Thank goodness I had moved those wine glasses.

He was a different person now. He had snapped. I stood there and he turned as if to go again, then came back with a barrage of abuse. He said it had been a crap week, he'd had a difficult week with the issues surrounding his wife, and now this. I thought he was going to leave. He turned and then stopped. He was like a man possessed, totally different from the person who had been shaking my hand a minute ago. By this time, I had my arm ready … I thought he was going to hit me. There was a lamp to my left, to his right, and he just punched it. The glass shattered all over the room.

As soon as Glenn Roeder and John Gorman heard that they steamed straight in and ushered Gazza out. When they came back John asked me if I was OK. I just said, 'I'm fine. We just need to get rid of this glass.'

Funnily enough, I don't think I had the most difficult job that day. I sympathized with everyone who was involved in trying to calm Gazza down enough to get him to the airport. I'm sure that the flight home, which Steve Double, part of our media staff, was in charge of, must have been terrible. It was never going to be the most enjoyable of days, and it was hardly surprising that there were a lot of emotionally exhausted people around the hotel that night. Gary Neville, in particular, was very upset for his brother.

I've thought long and hard about whether I handled breaking the news to the players in the right way. To be honest, I couldn't see any other way of doing it. It wouldn't have been right to line them all up and just say, 'Well you're not going and you're not going'. I didn't want to go to their rooms, either. Some people said I should have announced a squad of twenty-two, plus ten standby players, back in May before the Saudi Arabia game. But that could have caused resentment between certain of the players and what if some players had got injured?

In hindsight, I honestly feel I was right to handle it the way I did. The reaction of my twenty-two players the following day reinforced that belief. It was spot on. We had a really bubbly training session and I had a short chat with them in the middle of the pitch. I told them what a difficult day it had been for everyone connected with the squad, and what I expected of them over the next few days. Nothing major. I also mentioned our game against Tunisia for the first time. It seemed appropriate given that I had my actual squad together at last. By the end of that session I sensed a definite change within the camp: the feeling was more positive than negative, and players like David Beckham and Paul Scholes had come out of their shells.

Obviously, there was sadness for Gazza. It was only to be expected; they were close to him. But I think they realized, as I did, that while a fit Paul Gascoigne would have given us an added dimension, an unfit one would have been a disadvantage to the squad. When you're not fit it can take you a long time to get into a game. I couldn't include him on the basis of bringing him on with twenty minutes to go in the hope of him turning the game; it might take him twenty minutes to get into it. The bottom line was that I believed we now had a better squad than if Gazza had been included. That meant everything to me.

I still had to run the gauntlet of the media at the press conference. We'd put on a good show. The backdrop was magnificent and the sun was shining on the balcony which we'd redecorated with English flags. I was anticipating some tricky questions and knew it was being broadcast live back home. I remember saying a quick prayer beforehand, which I always do in situations like that.

Despite my worst fears, however, there was actually a lot of support for my decision and the questions were OK (except for the guy from Peperami TV; I still don't know what he was on about). In fact, as I was being asked questions, the answers were flowing in my mind. In the end, what could potentially have been one of the most difficult press conferences I've faced turned out to be one of the easiest and most enjoyable.

Not that I was bothered by what people thought. I had made the decision to leave Gazza out and that was that. I knew that not everyone would agree with me, but I admit I was disappointed by what Chris Waddle said about the situation. Chris is one of my oldest mates – we even made a record together if you remember. But what he said publicly about Gazza just weeks before the World Cup upset me. As for Rod Stewart and Chris Evans ... they just wouldn't understand.

Gazza's omission from my squad was the lead story on the national news that day. It seemed that the whole country wanted their say on the matter and emotions were running high. But it was all put into perspective for me when I walked into John Gorman's room after the last player had left my room. On the television there were distressing pictures of the earthquake in Afghanistan, including a mother and baby crying among the rubble. I just thought, 'Those six guys travelling to the airport might think their world is shattered, but it's nothing compared to that woman and baby.' Any negative feelings I had about what had just happened in the Royal Suite at La Manga went away pretty quickly after that.

PART TWO

CHAPTER 5

DANGER DAYS

1 JUNE – 8 JUNE 1998

As I boarded the plane at Murcia airport for the flight back to Luton, I felt satisfied with a job well done. Our trip to La Manga was never destined to be an easy one, but we'd got through it as well as I could possibly have hoped. The next major hurdle was the real thing: our opening first-round fixture against Tunisia in Marseilles, now just fourteen days away. We were almost there.

It had been an emotionally tiring few days and I could have done with some time to relax during the flight. But there was more work to be done: we still had to finalize our schedules for La Baule. There were training and travelling times to be sorted out, and I also wanted to make sure we had time to watch some of the other group matches being played in Nantes, of which Brazil against Morocco stood out. There was the press to accommodate, too. I'd started filling in the timetables for each day on the way out to Spain but there was so much to fit in that I hadn't finished. It was going to be non-stop out in France. I knew we weren't going to have a minute's peace.

I was particularly keen to get the schedules done and dusted before we touched down at Luton because I knew how much all of us – players and staff – needed a few days' break from football once we got home. We'd been away for two weeks and would be away for another five weeks after that ... all being well.

The plane was pretty quiet on the flight home. Not everyone had to work as I did, but perhaps they were taking a breather after the rollercoaster ride over the last few days. Then again, it could have had something to do with the fact that there was no drinks trolley to distract the players. I'd made it clear to them that alcohol was off limits while we were travelling. Alcohol is detrimental to an athlete at the best of times, but particularly during the recovery period immediately after a match, and during a flight, when the body dehydrates faster than normal. Once the body has had time, the odd drink won't do anyone any harm; in fact, it's probably good for team spirit. But I wasn't going to allow drinking on the plane at any time while we were travelling in France and I wanted the players to get used to that.

As far as English players – and particularly the older ones – are concerned, it's a case of old habits die hard. Traditionally, you play, you win and then you celebrate. More often than not, that can be damaging.

I don't want people to get the wrong idea and think that I rule the England players with an iron rod. Quite the opposite; it's very relaxed in the camp as the players will tell you. They are adults, after all. But I do feel very strongly about this issue, and that's why there was no drink on the plane.

In any case, I had a hunch that things might be difficult enough when we arrived at Luton. I was fully expecting another media circus wanting to talk about Gazza and I could not be sure how the public would react. There's always at least one person who over-reacts, and I thought we might have to have our wits about us. I was right.

It was all quite civilized at first. We collected our bags and emerged into the departure lounge, where we were separated from the public by barriers (we had learned our lesson from the overwhelming size of the welcoming party that greeted us after that match in Rome). I was looking out for my driver Ray Cousins, who was taking John Gorman and myself home, but all I could see were masses of people wishing us good luck and asking for autographs, which I signed as I moved along the barriers.

Unfortunately there were also plenty of television cameras and press photographers too, one of whom unintentionally sent John sprawling. It was nothing more than I'd expected, but I admit I was slightly unnerved by one journalist who kept shouting, 'Any reaction to the public backlash, Mr Hoddle?' I just smiled. 'I did my press conference in La Manga,' I said, continuing to sign autographs while trying to make some headway through the crowds. But it started to get frenzied and I lost sight of Ray, who was pushing the trolley carrying my bags. When I reached what I thought was my car, it turned out to contain our masseur, Steve Slattery. It was his car, not mine! In desperation I had to enlist the help of a policeman to escape the mayhem of autograph hunters, children falling over my feet and cars dropping off and picking up passengers outside the terminal building. I was mightily relieved to eventually escape the chaos by diving into Ray's car and driving off, with the photographers still clicking from every angle.

We had a bit of a laugh about it, but after about five minutes, it just hit me: this is a game of football we're talking about and I'm just a coach who made a decision to leave out a player. What we had just been through was mayhem.

By this time I was looking forward to escaping the media glare and having some time off over the next three days. But before that – late on the Monday night – I got a call from David Davies marking my card about an exclusive the *Sun* was to publish the following day in which Gazza was going to tell his side of the story.

I'd half-expected it. Gazza presumably had a contract with one of the tabloids for the duration of the World Cup, and now that he wasn't going he was under pressure to tell his side of the story. But, if I suspected that he might have a go at me, I was wrong.

Instead, he shot himself in the foot. I had protected him to the hilt, had chosen not to reveal things I could have during the press conference at La Manga, but Gazza told all: that he'd been drinking on the Saturday night, and again on the Sunday. Unfortunately, the article suggested I'd left him out for drinking reasons, which wasn't the case. But I think that anyone who started to read that still doubting my decision to drop him must have finished it understanding why I had no choice.

Still, it didn't bother me what people thought, I was more concerned with making the most of my few days off. Once, that is, I had made some phone calls to solicitors and accountants about my continuing domestic problems. On that Tuesday I saw Vanessa, briefly, then later that afternoon two of my kids, Jamie and Zara (the eldest, Zoe, was away at a friend's house), and then went over to Eileen and Phil Drewery's house, where I was staying.

It was great to spend some time with the children; I'd missed them, of course, and I knew they'd missed me. We had a meal together and I helped them – or like to think I did – with their homework. But inevitably, the privacy didn't last long. My kickabout in the yard with Jamie attracted the attentions of a *Sunday Mirror* reporter who immediately came up the garden path to ask me for a quote on 'the Paul Gascoigne situation'. I told her that I had no comment, that I was spending some time with my kids. Under the circumstances I think

I was fairly polite!

My rebuttal didn't deter the three photographers who, despite the awful weather, appeared outside the house early the next day. One stood on the corner of the property, forcing Eileen's husband Phil to go out and tell him it was private and that the police would be round unless he moved his car. He did so, came back, and stood on the corner of a bend in a country lane getting absolutely soaked. All that to get one shot of me coming out of the house and getting into my car. The lengths these people will go to in order to get a not very exciting picture are incredible.

But none of this intrusive behaviour spoiled my time with the kids, who were full of beans and really excited about the start of the World Cup. They gave me good luck cards when I dropped them back home later that evening. Naturally, Anne and I had things to talk about. It was obviously a difficult time for her and the kids at home, and for Vanessa too. It was not all that easy for me, either, but I was just concentrating on the football at that point. They knew that was the way it had to be.

Later on, I caught up with a few mates at one of my locals, the Stag and Hounds in Binfield near Ascot. I've never been bothered in there before by anybody other than the odd auto-graph hunter, but obviously things are a bit different when the World Cup is just around the corner. The landlord put us in a separate bar which we had all to ourselves for the night and it was good to chill out, have a few beers and talk foot-ball – but not all the time. Like all good friends – I've known my mate Dave Deller for fifteen years – they know there's a time and a place. Dave's always been hot on the jokes and he didn't let us down that night. He was on top form.

My mum and dad were my priority on the Wednesday. My mum had celebrated her sixty-third birthday while we were in La Manga, but all my efforts to get something arranged for her had been in vain. So I took her out that after-noon to Ford's in Harlow where my brother Carl works, and bought her a car. It made two people happy: Carl with his commission, and my mum with her brand new Renault Clio!

I'm close to Carl, even though he's nine years younger than me, and was obviously disappointed that his football career never really took off. He and mum would be coming out for the Romania game. My dad prefers to watch the games in the comfort of his own home, which would probably be better for my mum's health too. She's a great worrier, and watching the game as the mum of the England coach creates a lot of pressure!

The public, meanwhile, obviously couldn't wait for the pressure to start. Wherever I went they wished me luck. Vanessa and I had a nice meal at the Canteen in Chelsea Harbour on the Wednesday night. It was a late night, made later by the amount of people who kept coming up to offer their support. It was the same the next day at Chessington World of Adventures with my children, which I had expected. But that was a smashing day too.

I was a bit naughty and sneaked the kids out of school as a treat in the hope of avoiding the crowds. Chessington wasn't as busy as it is at the weekends, but it was still full of school trips and I kept being asked for autographs and pictures. Eventually, I had to explain that if I had one photo done I'd have to do fifty and would be at it all day. It was the first time I'd ever done that, but I felt strongly about it. I have such limited time with the kids, and it might have been another five weeks before I saw them properly again.

The rain was considerate enough to hold off and we made the most of the day by going on all the rides, me included. I don't mind admitting that The Vampire was terrifying, although there was no way I was letting the kids see how I felt! But a smashing day was spoilt somewhat by a call I got during the afternoon from my adviser Dennis Roach informing me that one of the papers had got hold of a story involving Teddy Sheringham. I wasn't too pleased at having to deal with that on my day off, particularly as the kids were waiting for me.

When I was first told the story, I thought I wasn't hearing right. I could accept that Teddy had gone to Portugal but not that he'd been drinking in a bar until 6 a.m., not after what I'd categorically told the players before we went our separate ways after La Manga. I'd reminded them that they were still on World Cup duty and that they had to be careful what they did. By all means go out with your families, I said. Go to a restaurant, have a meal, see your friends … but forget night-clubs, especially in the small hours. They are out of bounds. A member of the public could take a snap of you and the press will be on to you like a flash. Don't take the risk.

In the back of my mind, of course, I was remembering Hong Kong and the infamous dentist's chair that caused so much trouble for England before Euro '96. I didn't want my World Cup preparations to be upset by a similar escapade.

I also couldn't believe that having identified the three days as a danger time as long as six months ago – we knew there was nothing going on and that we might need a story to keep the press happy – here we were playing into their hands. It was a spectacular own goal.

The players were due to join up at Bisham Abbey at 1 p.m. on the Friday but two hours before that I had a scheduled press conference with the Sunday papers, BBC and ITV. I had been keen to get it out of the way so I could focus on the next few days, but all of a sudden it didn't look like such a good idea after all.

Still, they soon realized there was no way I was going to talk about the incident until I'd seen Teddy face-to-face and got the full story, which I did an hour later in room 104 at our Burnham Beeches hotel. I was absolutely furious with him. At least he was honest enough to admit that he'd been out late at a club, but he said he wasn't drunk. I think I believed him. But he'd been unprofessional, and I told him so in no uncertain terms. His whole reaction told me he feared I was going to drop him from the squad and send him home.

That, however, was never going to happen. I'd checked the FIFA ruling – you couldn't drop a player and replace him unless he was injured – and anyway, I would have been cutting off my nose to spite my face. Teddy is a quality player who'd always been immaculate under me, both on the training ground and on the pitch. He'd never given us a single problem. Why should the England team, and our country's hopes suffer?

But what could I do? I couldn't leave him out and send him home, and it would have been absolutely pointless to fine him or take away his appearance fees. No, he needed to learn his lesson so in the end I decided that the most effective punishment would be to make him explain his actions – and apologize for them – to the public. 'I can't understand why you did what you did,' I told him, 'and neither can the public. So you are going to go out and tell them.' I think that was the harshest punishment I could have given him.

To be fair to Teddy, he took it on his chin – he's a strong character. I watched him closely over the next few days and it didn't affect his training. If anything, he seemed to go out on a limb and train even harder. It was totally different to the scenario with Gazza – he'd had numerous chances to get himself into shape and hadn't taken them. Teddy had stepped out of line once, and had apologized. There was no comparison.

We waited until the Saturday before we put out the apology because we were concerned that a follow-up to the story would appear in the Saturday papers. Of course, some of the press jumped the gun and criticized me for not reacting immediately, claiming that I'd lost any respect I'd gained over the way I'd dealt with Gazza. Paul McCarthy even claimed in the *Express* that we weren't going to react at all, that Teddy wasn't even going to appear, which was never the case. In hindsight, we did the right thing. The story was dead and buried by the Sunday morning.

However, by that time another story had surfaced about Darren Anderton allegedly being involved in a scuffle in a bar. Almost before I'd had time to take this in, Darren called me. Apparently, he'd gone out with his family and friends to a restaurant to celebrate getting into the squad after all his setbacks. Afterwards they'd gone into a bar across the road to have a few beers and a fight broke out. Darren had had nothing to do with it. He wasn't even there when it started, and certainly wasn't drunk. In other words, it was a load of hot air. We put a statement out very quickly saying exactly that, and the story never took off.

I still felt extremely deflated on that Friday however, as if the wind had been taken out of my sails. I felt let down, I really did. I had gone to such lengths to make sure we didn't have to deal with these kinds of problems, and Teddy's mistake had gone and ruined it. So there I was having to talk about the incident when I should have been discussing training sessions, shapes and tactics. It was a waste of time and energy.

I knew that such hassles were inevitable, and that I couldn't show my feelings. I had to put on a performance for that televised Friday press conference. And by the Sunday, when it had all blown over, I was more at ease with myself and could start looking forward again.

Chicago was our destination on the Saturday evening – the musical version in the West End of London, that is! We took the players and their wives and girlfriends to the theatre. The idea was for everyone to get to know one another before they met again in France for the game against Colombia on 26 June (by which time, hopefully, we would have qualified for the last sixteen). We'd planned the trip for a while and it had been quite difficult to decide on an appropriate activity, bearing in mind we were catering for everyone from eighteen-year-old Michael Owen to Doc Crane, who's sixty-nine. But John Gorman and his wife had seen the production and recommended it, although I don't think they mentioned that it was about women getting their own back on men! Anyway I didn't believe you could go far wrong with a jazz production, although I suspect one or two of the younger players did find it a bit heavy-going. I thought I noticed Paul Scholes nodding off two rows in front of me.

We had a nice meal afterwards at Christophers restaurant and finished off with a great karaoke going home on the bus. John Gorman sung his version of 'My Way' and the Doc spun out a couple of jokes. But the highlight of the evening was emerging from the theatre at 11 p.m. to find hundreds of people cheering us and chanting 'Football's Coming Home'. The players were absolutely gobsmacked. It certainly reminded us – if we needed reminding – just how much England doing well in the World Cup means to the public. It was a real eye-opener.

It was a good night to name-drop, too. Dani Behr was there with Les Ferdinand, while Victoria Adams flew in to join us at the buffet lunch on the Sunday morning. She and David Beckham seemed very happy together. I began to suspect that David's mobile phone bill would be bigger than any other player's during the tournament.

Saying goodbye to the wives and girlfriends on the Sunday afternoon wasn't easy, particularly for the likes of Nigel Martyn, whose wife was expecting a baby three days before our first game. Nigel came to see me way before the squad was even picked and explained the situation – we would let him return for the birth and fly back to rejoin the squad afterwards. It may have been the World Cup, but some things are more important than football.

There was some dressing up to be done as well: organizing suits and sunglasses for the players and staff. Our suits are sponsored by Paul Smith, who also designed the suits for

Euro '96. I'd met him during my Chelsea days and we'd got on well. He's a big football fan and was the perfect choice to style our World Cup look. We'd been discussing colour schemes and styles for several months and had had a few half-hearted battles over it. I was always keen on something more summery than a dark suit and eventually got my way with beige. The blue suede shoes just added the finishing touch to the look (though everyone had brown leather shoes as well).

I was really pleased with how smart everyone looked. It was the World Cup after all, and we were doing something to distinguish ourselves as a team. It was all part of the preparation. When I played for England we had blazers, shirts and ties that did nothing for the image of our country. Thankfully we've progressed from that.

But all this off-the-pitch activity hadn't distracted us from making progress where it really mattered, out on the training pitch. The music we used during our half-hour warm-up sessions lifted morale (John got a range of tapes compiled by the likes of London's Capital Radio, our videoman Gary Guyan, and even my twelve-year-old daughter Zara), and we put in some really hard work and worthwhile sessions before the Saudi game and again out at La Manga. The football we played in Casablanca gave us a really good base as well. We needed that in the tank. But from now on training would be less intense – eighty minutes at most – and we'd be toning it down even more the nearer we got to the tournament.

By then, however, we would have worked on every aspect of our game. On that last day before leaving for France, we did a lot of work on pressing the ball as a team, something which I didn't feel we'd been doing as well as I'd have liked, particularly at Wembley. It's all about hunting the ball collectively, closing down the opposition when they have the ball so they have limited space to play into. I worked on it with the team that would be starting in Caen and they seemed to have grasped the concept, but I haven't see us do it often enough during a game. We would keep hammering it down the players' throats until we were absolutely sure they knew what they were doing. If we got it right in the World Cup it would really give us an edge.

We'd been doing a lot of work on our counter-attacking too – putting the players into two teams of eight and giving each individual a different function on the pitch. We'd then start with one eight in possession of the ball. They would have six passes with which to try to keep possession, try to break the other team down and wait to cut through them. When they've had six passes, their time for being patient is over, and they would have to score within fifteen seconds. Meanwhile, their opposition would be trying to gain possession. If they did, they would have to score within fifteen seconds.

Some individuals – Les Ferdinand, Paul Ince and Darren Anderton – needed a bit of extra physical training too but in general the players were in excellent shape. That was more than could be said for me. I pulled my calf muscle while we were out in La Manga, which meant that I was already ruled out of a game on the Monday between the press and the staff. In the end the game had to be called off. Too many of the press had already left for France, and Terry Byrne and Gary Lewin, our manager and coach, were distraught. They had been arguing over what formation to play, and over who was going to play wing-back and sweeper – I wasn't the only one with decisions to make – and trying to persuade Ray Clemence to play in goal. Ray's excuse for refusing was that he'd lost his gloves; more likely he just wanted to play out-field and take a few scalps!

We planned to rearrange the game for when we were in France, depending on whether or not the press boys would give us a fair crack of the whip. There were a few members of the press we wanted to put one over on the pitch, that was for sure!

On that Monday, too, I was chuffed to receive a fax from the England cricket captain Alec Stewart wishing us luck and saying, 'Go and win it for us all.' It's nice to have that bond between cricket and football – we resolved to return the favour when they played their Test matches against South Africa. It was another reminder of the responsibility we were carrying with us to the World Cup, the start of which was now just two days away.

During our final training session at Bisham Abbey there was a farcical moment just as I was preparing to wind the session up. It transpired that the man from Peperami TV, who had been at our La Manga press conference a week earlier, had travelled over from Spain. Out of the corner of my eye I noticed this great big Peperami coming out of the bushes and across the pitches with a ball under its arm! He interrupted me in mid-sentence and said something like, 'Any chance of a game?' Then, 'Can I just take a throw-in?' I left John Gorman to sort him out!

I saw the funny side of it afterwards, but I have to admit I was amazed he'd managed to get on to the pitch (we train as far from the road as possible – across at least two football pitches) despite the presence of so many security people. After all, he was difficult not to notice! Our security men, Ray Whitworth and Terry Wise, took some horrendous stick, I can tell you. When Ray caught up with him he said, 'Get your head off. I'm not standing here talking to a sausage!'

Following that episode I was pleased that the final press conference afterwards concentrated on football. We were done with talking about the problems of Gazza, Teddy, Darren and even Mr Peperami. Now the press wanted to know how excited I was, and how confident I really felt.

I could honestly tell them I felt very positive, that I'd prepared the players for seven games, and that I certainly didn't intend coming back after three. I told them, too, that we had left no stone unturned in our preparation, and that I felt this squad was better prepared than any of its predecessors. I meant it.

Those last few days at home – sorting out the problem Teddy had created, finishing off our training, and, as important, building a real feeling of togetherness amongst the players, the staff, and all our families and those closest to us – had been memorable in their own way.

I think we managed to do it all. It really pleased me to see how well everyone got on together over the weekend at Burnham Beeches, especially the wives and partners. There were plenty of laughs, and there was a real feeling of excitement made all the more real by that fantastic reception in London on Saturday night.

It was a proud time for all of us. I saw the pride in the faces of the coaches, John and Clem and Peter Taylor and Glenn Roeder. They are all real professionals but representing your country at a World Cup is like nothing else.

The great thing about my relationship with John Gorman is that we bounce off each other, and we don't mind each other's company over long periods of time, which is vital in this job. We've never had an argument all the time we've been together. There are times when we disagree – that's all part of a healthy working relationship – but we've never fallen out. The closest we got was when he stayed at Swindon after saying he was coming with me to Chelsea.

John's got a great football brain, great enthusiasm and a wonderful way with the players. He's a caring man who gets involved in their personal situations, and often talks to them on the phone between matches. He's also managed a club himself so he's got experience, but I think he just loves being out on that training ground. His enthusiasm rubs off on the players, which is an absolutely priceless quality. He also does a lot behind the scenes to help take the pressure off me – his loyalty has been such a help over the last two years. We are great mates and have so much respect for one another.

It's a pleasure working with him.

Ray Clemence was a top keeper in his time with Liverpool and Spurs, and at the time I took over as England coach The F.A. needed a respected goalkeeping coach. His knowledge has been invaluable to me, but not just on the goalkeeping side. He's got a lot of experience, both as a player and a manager, and he's got strong opinions on everything from squad selections down to the nitty-gritty of defending corners and set-plays. He's very upfront, but he's got a great sense of humour too and is always getting involved in wind-ups. When you're working in each other's pockets you need someone like that around. He's worked very closely with David Seaman, Ian Walker, Tim Flowers and Nigel Martyn over the last two years and I think he's enjoyed growing as a coach during that time.

Peter Taylor is a very funny guy – his Norman Wisdom impression is legendary – but he's also an extremely organized coach. The problem he has is that people might misconstrue his intentions. One minute he's having a laugh and a joke – he and Alan Shearer like to have a bit of a banter every day – and the next he's taking a spot-on training session. He's still got the mind of a player in many ways, which is probably why the players respond to him so well. I picked him to manage the Under-21s because I knew that with his character, personality and coaching ability, he'd be perfect for the job. I think players at that level need a manager who is on their wavelength. If you talk about the old days too much then players will switch off. I like the balance between Peter and Dave Sexton.

Glenn Roeder has been involved with us from the very beginning. He scouted for us for the first eight or nine months and did a fantastic job. I like Glenn because he's had the experience of being a manager himself, plus he's been a number two, to Chris Waddle at Burnley. Like all the people around me he was an excellent technical player and he's

handed on his experience to the players. I think that's important in a coach. He's a very upright, honest guy who took a bit
of time to settle into the job, but we kept him ticking over and
he's had a tremendous input, both as a scout and as a coach.

The great thing about all four of them is that I can dele-
gate. I can say, you take that warm-up for fifteen minutes, or
you split the group into three, and they will go and do it
while I focus on the main bulk of the training. The five of us
also work well together in that Glenn and John were both
attacking defenders, Peter and I were attacking midfield
players, and Ray saw the game for all those years from the
back; you learn so much from there. So I feel we've got the
balance right, both in terms of expertise and of personalities.

I didn't tell that last press conference, however, about the
dream I'd had the previous night, in which England had
reached the final against Brazil, but without Paul Ince, who
had been sent off in the tunnel beforehand. I had no idea why –
perhaps it was a new FIFA directive! I also chose not to
reveal my innermost thought, which was that England would
win the World Cup. I really believed that. We'd waited so
long for the tournament, and prepared so well. In my mind,
there was no other possible outcome.

CHAPTER 6

BIENVENUE A FRANCE

9 JUNE – 14 JUNE 1998

I wanted a good send-off the day we left England for our World Cup adventure; nothing over the top, but something that would boost the players and that everyone would remember. I knew using any of the normal airport terminals would be chaotic. Instead, British Airways offered us what they call their engineering depot. What seemed like thousands of their staff turned out. When our police escort brought the coach in, they erupted. Hundreds of BA staff came on to the runway. They clapped every player as he got off the coach to board the plane. That's when it really hit us … where we were going and why we were going there. There was a real buzz. And as we took off, I remember looking down over the green fields and thinking: 'I hope I don't see you again until 13 July.'

Tuesday 9 June was always going to be a big day in my life. It was the day for which I had been preparing for the last two years. After all the months of planning and preparation, we were at last on our way to France and the World Cup.

My good mood improved during the flight when I saw the team picture in some of the papers, including *The Times* and the *Telegraph*. I don't remember a team picture getting such coverage before. Naturally, there were some favourable remarks and some derogatory ones about our suits, but the general feeling was that we all looked really smart.

We weren't flying straight to our base at La Baule, but stopping off to the north-east at Caen, where we were due to play a practice match against the French Second Division side. Unsurprisingly, it was pouring with rain as we touched down in France, although the poor visibility didn't prevent me from noticing what looked suspiciously like a sniper, perched on the roof of Caen's stadium near the entrance to the car park where our coach was heading. I have to admit I panicked for a moment. He was wearing a hooded jacket and I didn't know if he was a cop, a security man, or someone intending to have a pop at us. When he ducked behind a block of concrete and emerged with his machine gun pointed straight at our coach as it drew in, my heart missed a beat. I wasn't the only one, but luckily Peter Taylor kept a cool head. 'OK gaffer, I'm your man. I'll go out first for Queen and country,' he said ... and he stepped out of the coach. He survived!

Peter's twenty-fifth wedding anniversary was coming up – some of the players had been helping him write a poem to mark the occasion beforehand – and I don't think his wife would have appreciated anything happening to him! As for me ... it was my first experience of how heavy and visible our security was going to be.

The game, played in pouring rain, had the value of giving fifteen of my players match practice (we hadn't played a game for almost two weeks). A late Paul Scholes goal won it for us. The worst moment was a diabolical tackle on Gareth Southgate, which had us all off the bench. Luckily, Gareth was OK, but it did justify my insistence beforehand that the game be played behind closed doors. However, I had reluctantly agreed to allow 200-odd people connected with the sponsors of the French side to watch the game.

The reason, despite what the press claimed, was not simply to try a few things out away from the public glare, although that was part of it. There had been much debate about whether the match would be a dress rehearsal for the real thing and whether I would field the line-up that would start against Tunisia the following Monday. The answer might have been yes – until Sol Campbell suffered a thigh problem and Graeme Le Saux was laid low by flu – but there was no way I was going to reveal the true significance of the line-up … if I could help it.

However, I had been just as concerned about the effect a partisan crowd might have had on the Caen players. Imagine how much harder they might have tried, how much more committed they might have been in the tackle had there been 25,000 fans cheering them on. I couldn't take that risk so close to the World Cup.

The 1–0 win was welcome, but the players looked leggy and the performance was lacklustre. However, I knew I had to get something positive out of it to lift the players. They needed to know, on the eve of the World Cup, that I had no worries, that I believed in them. Obviously, I'd been hoping for better results in all our warm-up games, but what I'd got was no more than I'd expected. Those games were never going to be a barometer of the real thing, although that's not to say they had no value. If nothing else, I learnt about Gazza and Darren Anderton's fitness; saw Michael Owen score his international debut goal; experimented with a back four; and worked on our counter-attacking. All of those things would be important once we got to the World Cup. But as far as the results went I wasn't too worried. They were irrelevant to a certain degree. What mattered was how we performed come

2.30 p.m. in Marseilles on 15 June, when the scenario would be completely different.

In the dressing room after the game, I sat the players down – by the looks on their faces they obviously thought they were in for a rollicking – and told them so. 'Remember,' I said, 'that you've had two-hour training sessions right up until this game and I'm delighted with the way you've trained; you've trained like world champions. You've also travelled today – as you did on the day of our two games in Casablanca – which you won't be doing during the World Cup. You'll soon start to feel the benefit of the supplements, and the energy and vitamin pills that Dr Rougier has been prescribing, and from now on our training sessions will be much shorter. By the time the Tunisia game arrives you'll be feeling much sharper, physically and mentally.'

I had to get that message across to reassure them – and it worked, because they seemed in really good spirits on board the coach en route to La Baule from Nantes airport (after an enthusiastic but very wet reception from both press and public). Perhaps it had something to do with the fact that the music that had played us into Rome last November – the M People track, 'Search For The Hero Inside Yourself' – was on the cassette. Arriving at La Baule, and the Hotel Du Golf, did feel like coming home, as I'd expected. We had happy memories … and high hopes.

The Scots were due to take centre-stage in the opening game of the World Cup against Brazil on Wednesday 10 June. Kick-off for us, of course, was still five days away. But the excitement I felt about the start of the tournament was tempered somewhat by the Sky news bulletin which greeted me on that Wednesday morning with reports of crowd disturbances on the streets of Paris around the Champs-Elysées. Unfortunately, football will still get the blame, even though the problem seemed to lie with French hooligans unconnected to the sport.

Dr Jan Rougier joined us in the morning. He gave the players his first detailed talk on their diet, and what a difference it can make over a five-week tournament. Then it was on to our opening training session at L'Escoublac. After all our worries, the pitch was perfection. Admitting several hundred local children and signing plenty of autographs also went down well. The children enjoyed cakes and drinks in our media hospitality tent, too. It was a good start on the public relations front. We didn't have a press conference on the first day of the World Cup Finals – the English media had asked us not to because so many of them were up in Paris for the Scotland game.

Before we left England I had sent a fax to Craig Brown and his side wishing them luck. Ironically, Craig had been trying to get in touch with me at the same time to explain comments he'd made to the Scottish journalists that he was worried might be misinterpreted as a criticism of England. Apparently, he'd told the Scottish press out in France that he hadn't got any stories for either their back or front pages ... which some people took as a dig at the English, implying that we can always be relied upon for controversy. The fact that Craig was worried about it shows how sensitive he is. I really like him, and sincerely hoped Scotland would do well in France – except if they came up against England!

We all watched the opening game together via a special feed of the BBC's coverage at the hotel. I had insisted on it, telling the squad that we were going to start the tournament as a group, and that we were damn well going to finish it as a group too, hopefully by bringing that gold trophy home. However, the 2–1 defeat wasn't the start Scotland needed and I really felt for them. To have to play the world champions in the opening game of the World Cup is a huge task, although having said that, it's definitely the best time to face them. But the Scots did themselves lots of favours, and I was especially pleased for Colin Calderwood, who was with me at

Swindon. I remember playing alongside him at Torquay in the Coca-Cola Cup in front of 2,000 people. I bet he had to pinch himself when he walked out on to the pitch at the Stade de France.

At half–time, when it was 1–1, I kept remembering Arsène Wenger telling me he thought Brazil might lose. In the end, of course, they needed a lucky own goal – even if it was a wonderful run from Cafu and a great ball from Dunga to set it up. But it was cruel on Scotland who played as if they believed they could get something out of the game. I certainly never thought Brazil would have to rely on a goal like that to win the game. I've often wondered whether champions get more luck, or whether they make their own luck, and this game left me none the wiser.

John Gorman and I did an interview for the BBC at half-time in a room we'd specially allocated to the television people for live broadcasts. Des Lynam inevitably asked John about Scotland. John is always being reminded about his Scottish background even though he's been working with England and me for more than two years. He takes it in good spirits. He enjoyed the attention his background got to start with, but I know he's fed up with it now. It's not an issue with me. England is John's only team.

I don't think I've taken more than a couple of England training sessions in the rain in the past, so I couldn't really complain about having to end training earlier than intended on occasions because of the awful weather in northern France during our first week there. We couldn't even get to the hotel breakfast room on Thursday morning without getting drenched, and a warm-down in a monsoon wasn't what we needed four days before our 1998 World Cup debut. The forecast suggested that Marseilles would be windy when we played there, rather than the 90 degrees which is normal for the area in June.

The players had plenty to keep them amused when they weren't training. The games room, in particular, was a huge hit. It was like an arcade and they loved it, Michael and Rio especially, although I couldn't believe that they wouldn't get tired of it by the time we left. There was also a great golf course and a super swimming pool, which wasn't exactly enticing in bad weather. We would be putting the pool to good use for training purposes, however: stretching in the water is a great way to recuperate and relax the day after a game. Racehorses have been doing it for years, and they are like highly tuned athletes, after all. But we would have to wait and see what the weather would bring!

The first day in the media centre seemed to go OK. The only question that threw me a little came from a Russian journalist who wanted to know my feelings about the players and sex! One of the English press made the inevitable joke about 'only behind closed doors', referring to our practice match in Caen that some of the journalists kept going on about. There were fifteen camera crews at the press conference – you could feel the excitement building. The *Sun* wanted support for their campaign to get everyone back home a couple of hours off to watch the game against Tunisia. I thought it would happen anyway. What was happening at home was amazing although I wasn't surprised by it.

Of course I was delighted that the public were so behind us, but personally, I tried hard not to get carried away with the hype that inevitably surrounded our World Cup campaign. I tried not to read the papers – just the *Telegraph* occasionally – and I avoided the television as best I could, although that was more difficult with Sky News on all the time. I wanted to keep in touch with what the other teams were up to but when they started on England I went straight for the remote control. I also had to have a rethink about the television being available when the players were eating as it isn't helpful having a discussion going on about who should and who shouldn't play for England while they are chomping into their cereals.

The only way I can do this job is if I deal with what I have to – and nothing else. If I'm tired, it's because I'm putting all my energies into training, and into the logistics of the job. There are a million and one questions to be answered every day and I don't need to be affected by other people's opinions. I know what I want from my team, I listen to the people I respect and work with and I make my decisions on the back of that. It annoyed me to be told that Kevin Keegan had had a pop at me – I think it was over my squad selection – in one of the papers earlier in the week. But I've been in this business long enough to know that Kevin is only saying these things because people are paying him to, which I understand. It's all about opinions, and everyone's entitled to theirs. But as England coach, mine is the one that matters when it comes to picking who plays and who doesn't.

What's interesting about sport, and life in general, is that everyone focuses on what they don't agree with rather than what they agree with. They never say, 'That was a great decision.' There might be eight decisions that they agree with and one that they don't, and it's the one that they don't agree with that they concentrate on. That's the one the media focus on. That's the one that Joe Public focuses on. And that reality is the hardest part of this job. I've always maintained that there are three games of football going on. There's one from up in the stand – from the press or season-ticket position; one from the bench; and one from the pitch, from the player's perspective. Just because you've sat up in the stands for twenty years watching games doesn't necessarily give you the experience needed to pick a team. I would love to put an experienced reporter out in the centre circle and get him to report a game from there. He would write a totally different match report.

But as long as there's praise when it's due then I can take the criticism. It's all part of the job. What I do object to are people who have been in my shoes being critical for the sake of it. Bobby Robson took the time to call me and say he was right behind me, that he'd give me all the support he could. As for Terry Venables ... I wasn't sure. I think it has been difficult for Terry during the two years that I have been head coach. I'm sure he feels that he should still be in the job. So I would have to wait and see.

Dealing with the media wasn't my main task that first Thursday in La Baule, because that was the day I chose to inform the players who was in the starting line-up to face Tunisia. I did it at the training ground after our morning session four days before match day. I sat them all down in the centre circle and went through all the reasons why some players were in and some were out. Of course a few were disappointed, especially Becks. Their faces and eyes gave it away to both me and John, who was watching them closely. That's human nature. But I stressed to them that this tournament was all about twenty-two players; that matches could be won and lost in the last twenty minutes of a game, so substitutes were just as important as the starting eleven. I asked them, too, whether they thought any team would go through this World Cup and finish a match with exactly the same eleven players who started it. The unanimous answer was no.

I asked the players not to reveal the starting line-up. Keep it from your families until we get to Marseilles, I said. I don't want agents knowing, either. Don't let your team mates down. Don't let anyone down. I told them to go into that afternoon's press conference and say the team hadn't been named, which was officially true. The great thing about our training ground at L'Escoublac was that it was so private – anyone trying to get in would literally have to climb up ladders and over walls – so I know that my team selection would stay a secret ... if everyone kept their word.

What I wasn't going to do at this stage was throw in any red herrings. It wasn't worth it yet. If we had reached the quarter-finals, I might have considered broadcasting the fact that so-and-so had gone down with an injury and it was a big blow, when we knew full well that he'd be playing. I knew I wouldn't be the only coach playing those games.

As for my team selection I felt strongly that it was important to give the players a few days to come to terms with it so that by Monday, by the time we got to Marseilles and kick-off, the spirit in the camp would be spot on again. I couldn't afford to have players sulking around because they weren't playing. I know how damaging that can be to team morale. In the World Cup in Spain in 1982 there were a couple of players in the England squad carrying slight injuries who felt they should be playing, and the spirit wasn't right as a result. What happens off the pitch is just as important as what happens on it, and we would be doing lots of work on the players who weren't playing this time, talking to them and keeping them upbeat. But the harsh reality of being a footballer is that while there may be twenty-two of you working together, at the same time there are twenty-two players competing against each other, too. You have to be selfish, you have to think, 'I don't care about anyone else, I want to be in the team.' That should be the attitude of every pro.

I knew that my team selection would probably surprise a few. Since I've been England coach I've had so much criticism from people – telling me to name my strongest line-up and stick with it, that I'm tinkering with the side too much, who to play and how to play them – so let me set the record straight. I have known my most experienced side for some time, but I've seldom had the chance to play it (even in Rome we were without Alan Shearer). I also knew that that team could do the business for me given the chance.

But I vividly recall coming away from Le Tournoi last year and realizing that we could actually have beaten Brazil in our third game. We got it right against them tactically. We got through their midfield with some ease but our wing-backs, Graeme Le Saux and Phil Neville, didn't have fresh enough legs to support our front players. Had they been less tired I'm convinced we could have caused them all sorts of problems. It was a defining moment for me. I realized that if we progressed in the World Cup we could end up playing games in the later stages with a far less experienced team than I'd bargained for, what with suspensions and injuries on top of loss of form.

That's when I knew that at some stage during the build-up to the World Cup I would have to look very seriously at Michael Owen up front; I'd have to consider David Beckham in the middle of the park; I'd have to compare Paul Scholes and Steve McManaman in the playmaker's role. I wanted to get to the stage where I could say, facing a quarter-final against, for example, Germany, 'Well, I've lost David Batty through suspension but so-and-so is equally capable in his place.' I knew that by then I had to be sure what my options were, know exactly who had the temperament for the big occasion, and who didn't.

If I'm totally honest, I still wasn't sure whether I had enough options. At the highest level it's all about being assured enough to go out on the pitch and reproduce what you do on the training ground. Your Sheringhams and your Shearers, your Seamans and your Inces and your Adams ... they all do that. David Batty's getting there. Players like Gary Neville, Sol Campbell and Gareth Southgate are on the way. Paul Scholes is the player who has recently impressed me the most. He just gets on with it. He reproduces his club form for his country every time, but I can't be absolutely sure about everyone.

Certainly, there were times during our build-up when I thought certain players would perform better than they did. Gazza was one. And David Beckham was another who had yet to come alive and be more assured.

The fact that I left David out of the team to start against

Tunisia came as the biggest shock of all, particularly since I gave him his international debut and he started every one of our qualifying games. But I just felt that his club form dipped towards the end of the season and that he wasn't as focused and sharp as he might have been in our warm-up matches, especially against the Saudis. He'd been drifting in and out of too many games. His passing had sometimes fallen below his own very high standards. There had been a vagueness about him, on and off the pitch, and sometimes in training. I'm sure he was missing Victoria, who's away a great deal. As a result of all this, he was a bit distant around the hotel, wrapped up in his own problems. Darren Anderton had come in and played well at wing-back – I think he's a better player defensively than David and crosses the ball just as well – and has shown me a bit more willingness to play out wide. Basically, David prefers to play inside – it's his natural instinct to play more centrally. But when he does play out wide, he gives us good width, particularly with his ability to cross the ball.

I know my decision affected David. It really jolted him, as I knew it would. He was extremely disappointed, but I talked to him one-on-one and explained my reasons for leaving him out. I also told him that there were four reasons why I might change the line-up – injury, suspension, tactics and form – so it was up to him to keep himself mentally and physically ready to play. Don't think, well that's the team so that's it, I told him. He listened and seemed to half-agree with what I was saying. I thought – and hoped – he understood. He had several days to get over it and be ready to come on as sub if needed. I gave him permission to see his girlfriend the following day, which seemed to help him. Victoria flew into La Baule's airport and she and David spent several hours together at the local golf club on the Friday. He still had a part to play in the World Cup, that was for sure.

We'd always earmarked the golf club as a place where the

players could meet any family or friends who were over in France. I didn't feel it was right to let them into the hotel because if one or two players have family staying, and others don't, it could be disruptive. I wasn't surprised, however, when David and Victoria were spotted by the media saying goodbye at the airport. (It turned out to have been a fluke – a *Mirror* photographer happened to be there arranging to fly a good luck banner over the town.)

Sol Campbell, meanwhile, was also spotted by the media doing a bit of shopping in La Baule, which I'd given him permission to do rather than play golf like the rest of the squad. I warned him he might have to handle a bit of press, and sure enough, within half an hour there was a media call about why he was there.

Most of the other players joined in Friday morning's golf tournament, arranged by our golf secretary Ray Clemence. It was all laid on and very efficient – buggies, sponsored clubs, starting times, etc. The boys couldn't grumble about anything on that front – they were well looked after.

I was persuaded to let the photographers and cameras record the opening tee shots. To their delight, young Michael Owen and Teddy Sheringham were in the same group as Alan Shearer. Sheringham or Owen to partner Shearer up front was already exciting the journalists. Michael – who's probably the best golfer in the squad and plays off an eight handicap – made a hash of his drive. There was a bit of banter about that as you can imagine, and it definitely settled a few nerves among the less competent golfers in the party! Darren Anderton took the title off David Seaman, who had won the last time we all played. I had a great four with John Gorman against Brian Scott and Clem; I was desperately trying to beat Ray Clemence's score. Clem and I have had a long-standing battle on the golf course over the years – £10 on the front nine, £10 on the back nine and £10 for the game – and I was about four matches up in this trip. It was a difficult time for Clem! Let's hope it stays that way!

The golf was the only organized activity on the day I gave everyone twenty-four hours off from training. We hadn't had any free days since we got together on the Friday before flying to France and I thought everyone would benefit from the break. At least it gave us a chance to watch some World Cup action on TV. Some of the players watched all three of the games that day and our bookies – Alan Shearer and Teddy Sheringham – did good business in front of the big screen on results, first goalscorer, etc. Tony Adams took a shine to Paraguay but they let him down – and pleased the bookies – with a goalless draw against Bulgaria.

John Gorman and Glenn Roeder went into Nantes on the Saturday afternoon to see Nigeria beat Spain 3–2 in a smashing match. It just showed the progress African football has made but I hoped that Tunisia wouldn't follow suit on Monday. I was really looking forward to getting underway. I'd named the team. We'd worked on the game. We'd done the set-plays. I was positive and focused and couldn't wait for it to start.

I was confident I wouldn't get tense before the game but I'd probably get a few flutters on the way to the stadium. Once I'm cocooned in the dressing room my professional head comes on. The most nerve-wracking time for me is when we go out on to the pitch and the players step over that white line leaving me to turn right or left to the bench, or go up into the stands. I'm on edge. I'm thinking: 'Can they remember that? I hope he plays well. He's a key figure. Can we stop him playing? What pattern are they playing? Have we got enough width? Is our shape right? Do we adjust it?' Eventually, the game settles down but those first ten minutes are always the worst.

Since I've been England coach that period of a game has been even more nerve-wracking because I'm never entirely sure whether the players have taken on board what we've told them. They are a quieter, more thoughtful bunch of players that many I've known. They sometimes seem reluctant to speak out in front of one another, and there's not enough feedback, even from the experienced players. I want more. However, they are no different from most players in that they won't understand what you're trying to get across to them on theory alone; you have to get out on the training ground and practise what you've been preaching.

I did exactly that with our set-plays, which we'd been working on big-time for the last six months. We'd kept a lot of them under wraps since Rome and I had some fresh ideas to introduce the further down the line we went. We hadn't shown our hand at all. Games are so close nowadays that if you can score from set-plays you've got a hell of a chance. You need to be imaginative and I get ideas from watching Premiership matches week in, week out. You develop ideas and toss them around with the other coaches. Peter Taylor's very organized on set-plays and Ray Clemence's ideas of defending against them are excellent. I remember him organizing our defence fantastically at Tottenham. We all come up with ideas but in the end it's down to me. If we lost a goal because I'd left the explaining to someone else I'd never forgive myself. Now that would stop me sleeping at night.

Talking of sleeping, I fancied a lie-in like the players on the Sunday morning before our first match, but there were more important things on the agenda, namely an early phone call from the Prime Minister wishing us luck against Tunisia. When I was first told he was going to call I thought it was a wind-up by Steve Penk, the Capital Radio DJ. I'd already had a call from someone claiming to be the Archbishop of Canterbury (I told the caller that Mr Hoddle had gone to church!) – Alan Shearer and David Batty had got one too – so I was very sceptical when the PM's name was mentioned. I've been around too long to be caught out like that.

But this was no wind-up. It really was Tony Blair on the

end of the line telling me he was disappointed that he could-
n't watch the game because of a Summit meeting, but that
he'd organize a tea break at just the right time. He also
reminded me that the whole nation was behind us. It was a
good chat, even if it was the first time I became aware of the
troubles in Marseilles involving England fans, and we agreed
to talk again ... on the eve of the World Cup Final! Hopefully.

We were Marseilles-bound shortly after the call. The journey from our hotel to San Nazaire airport was lively, thanks
to a short video that Ian Wright had recorded before he left La
Manga. Wrighty beamed out from the screen – he'd taken his
shirt off and painted three lions on his chest – wishing us
luck and telling us to go and win it for England. He had a
lighthearted pop at David Davies about not worrying too
much, and at our masseur Steve Slattery ... something about
doing too much talking and not enough rubbing! Anyway,
the boys loved it. There were lots of laughs from the back of
the coach.

It said a lot about Wrighty's character that he'd done that
at a time when his World Cup dream had just been shattered.
I don't know whether it sunk in when he got back home or
not, but he certainly took it better than I have ever known
anyone take a similar setback. He didn't upset the spirit of
the camp one bit. I hoped he and Jamie Redknapp would
come out to join us as it would be good to have them around.

It was en route to the stadium for a training session that
Sunday night that we really discovered the extent of the trouble in Marseilles. Some of the roads had been blocked off and
we took longer than we should have done to get to the stadium. The police were blocking the road from the port area and
there were a lot of people just wandering aimlessly around. I
remember thinking, 'Here we go again'. It's so disappointing
that a minority of people can let the country down. I consider them idiots. The best solution has to be to stop them travelling, how ever that is done.

But we had to switch off from that to a certain extent, and I was relieved to reach the Vélodrome and get back to thinking about football. Personally, I couldn't wait to get out on to the pitch. It made me feel like we'd well and truly arrived at the World Cup. The first thing I did out there was say a prayer. I did the same in Poland, and in Rome, and I would be doing it on every pitch before every big game we played. It wasn't a prayer to win the game. It doesn't work like that. It's more like a positive vibration, asking for an energy to help overcome any negativity in the stadium.

Thankfully, there was nothing negative about the mixed-zone press conference that followed that training session. It was spot on, despite the fact that it was my debut on the World Cup media stage (outside our base) in front of 300 people from press, radio and television and I could have been forgiven a bit of stage fright. (Apparently, there were just twenty-six people at the Tunisian coach's press conference, so he got off lightly!) In fact, I really enjoyed it; it can be a battle of wits, trying to turn around some of the sticky questions they throw at you. I have got more used to it now and even enjoy the challenge of some press conferences.

The lighthearted tone was set from the start when David, an interpreter and I entered and stood in front of three microphones like the Three Degrees. Someone even shouted, 'I thought you were going to sing "Diamond Lights".' After all the joking, it was a shame the first question related to the overnight troubles, which I had to deflect diplomatically and move on to football-related matters. I couldn't be expected to know all the facts of what had happened. In those circumstances it was best to leave all comment to our security people. It's too easy just to condemn people who sometimes turn out to have been innocent. I also remember someone asking me which was more important: to entertain, or get a win. Of course I replied that we had to get a win, but that if we could entertain at the same time, so much the better. Would any coach, facing his first World Cup game and desperate for a winning start, say any different? I doubt it.

There was a wonderful spirit in the camp that night. Most of the players turned in early, before 11 p.m. Only Incey and Les Ferdinand, who both took the option of a late massage, stayed up. We'd watched the game between Jamaica and Croatia, which the Croatians won 3–1. It was a useful experience to see the Croatians in action since we'd be meeting either them or Argentina in the next round, depending on how the groups worked out. I thought then that Croatia could be a danger in this World Cup. Of course, we had scouts watching both teams, as well as the Germans, just in case. We had to be prepared to go all the way, otherwise we'd be risking getting caught out in what would probably be the most vital game of our lives.

The game against Tunisia was now just a matter of hours away. However, getting this far was not something I'd even allowed myself to dream about when I took over as England coach, just over two years ago. There had been so many hurdles to overcome beforehand that I couldn't just push the fast-forward button to the World Cup Finals. I mean, what if we hadn't qualified for France? I would have been hammered, that's what.

I will admit that I always thought the England job would come my way one day. I'd thought that since day one in management. Optimistically I had a get-out clause written into my contract at Swindon that would allow me to leave should it come up while I was at the County Ground, even though at that time in my heart I had no real desire to be England manager. At Chelsea, the same clause was there, yet I went there thinking, 'I don't even want the England job. It's a thankless task, all the baggage that goes with it.'

But having said that, I always felt that there was someone poking me, as if to remind me that it would come up one day. I never thought it would come up as quickly as it did, but when it did, I knew the time was right. Football in England is bigger than it's ever been, and I believed that the players we had – while they might not be the greatest technical players in the world compared to the likes of Brazil and even some of the African nations – were undoubtedly better players than England had been blessed with for some time.

I was also swayed by having the 1998 World Cup on our doorstep; likewise the 2000 European Championships which will be staged in Holland and Belgium. All in all, the arrow was only pointing in one direction: to the sign saying 'Do It'.

You can never plan how a job is going to turn out, but I feel very comfortable in the role. I do miss the day-to-day involvement of club management, but if I'm honest I like the periods when I can do other things. Don't get me wrong: this is a 100 per cent full-time job and I'm lucky if I can even squeeze in a game of tennis, but there are so many other things happening in my life that I need time to sort them out. Of course that wasn't possible during the World Cup, but France '98 was an unusual situation when life was put on hold.

I do believe that I'm a better coach now than I ever was at Swindon or at Chelsea, because I've got time to study players, to study games. It's like having an extra eye. In many ways I think I'm a better person, too, because I've had to be aware of everyone in the group, and take care of all the minor details as well as the major ones. One thing I've never been good at as a manager is forecasting results – I haven't had a good result at the bookies yet – but on the eve of our 1998 World Cup debut, I thought: 'It's going to be 1-0 – to England.' I would be happy with that.

CHAPTER 7

TUNISIA–A WINNING START

15 JUNE 1998

I felt incredibly focused and yet relaxed during our final squad meeting in the hotel before the Tunisia game. I could tell the players did too. We had done so much work on the training ground that all I needed to do was go over details to make sure the players were certain of our shape and our tactics. We illustrated key points on the board, and it was obvious to me, John and Clem – we were all watching the players intently – that every single one of those twenty-two players was concentrating on what I was telling them. It was all sinking in.

Match day had meant a 10 a.m. wake-up call, half an hour before that scheduled last chat, followed by brunch at 11 a.m. There was plenty of choice on the menu – fish, chicken, pasta, yoghurt, apple pie and fruit. The players had obviously taken Dr Rougier's advice on board – the proteins went down first to line the stomach, then the carbohydrates. It's not what most of them are used to, but these minor details

Joy, relief and pride – celebrating the final whistle in Rome on 11 October 1997, and qualification for the 1998 World Cup (above). The England team golf day in early May 1998 (left).

(ACTION IMAGES, ALLSPORT)

Pre World Cup training in La Manga (left). All the players loved La Manga. I found myself wishing I could pick it up and transport it to France.

At our opening match in the King Hassan II tournament against Morocco (below), the wrong national anthem was played for England. Our boys, led by Incey, Gazza and Wrighty, insisted on singing the right one. Good for them.
(ALLSPORT)

Paul Gascoigne coming off during the second half of our match against Belgium in the King Hassan II tournament. He had a dead leg and a cut head and sadly, just didn't look up to the task.

(ALLSPORT)

Michael Owen clashes with the Moroccan goalkeeper. He was out cold for a few seconds and his first words as he came round were 'I don't want to come off, I won't come off.' He went on to score the winner.

(ALLSPORT)

On the way to the training ground in La Manga. Michelle Farrer, our international administration assistant, is on my right.

(TIM SONNEX)

The medical men. Back row left to right: Terry Byrne, John Crane, Steve Slattery. Front row left to right: Alan Smith, Tim Sonnex and Gary Lewin.

Our final press conference in La Manga (above). I thought it was going to be one of the most difficult conferences I've faced but it turned out to be one of the easiest and most enjoyable. During our final training session before leaving for France (right), John Gorman had to see off a late visitor, the infamous Peperami man.

Proud and excited to be representing our country (above left). We finally left for France on 9 June. We all hoped we wouldn't be back until 13 July.

Alan Shearer and Paul Scholes made excellent starts to our campaign by scoring the winning goals in our opening match against Tunisia (above and left).

(ALLSPORT, EMPICS, ACTION PLUS)

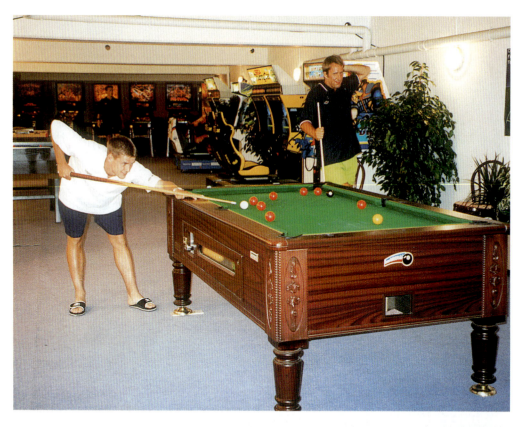

Michael Owen and
Paul Merson made
good use of the
facilities in our
temporary home in
La Baule (above).
While travelling
between matches,
our doctor John
Crane and our physio
Alan Smith would
usually take the
opportunity to catch
forty winks! (right)

(TIM SONNEX)

were crucial to our preparation. (It's not what the coaching staff are used to either; there were some interesting discussions during the brunch about match-day meals of the past. I certainly remember some spectacular blow-outs, including steak and chips!)

Fortunately, we didn't have too much time to kill after the meal. Kick-off in Marseilles was at the rather unusual time of 2.30 p.m. and we were due to leave our hotel – the Sofitel near Marseilles airport – at midday. I put it back to 12.10 p.m., knowing we'd probably be away by 12.15 p.m. I never like to arrive at the ground more than an hour and a half before kick-off. We have a deliberately tight pre-match schedule that suits us. There's nothing worse than hanging around a dressing room waiting an age until the start of the game.

Had we not watched the Sky News bulletins in the hotel, we would never have known about the overnight trouble on the streets of Marseilles. The pictures were terrible. On the one hand, you don't want to make any excuses for English hooligans. On the other hand, the pictures – and the security advice that David Davies was getting – said it clearly wasn't only their fault. The evidence I saw with my own eyes on the TV screen certainly suggested there were many trouble-makers who certainly didn't appear to be English.

All the players I'm sure had seen what I'd seen on the TV. But it hadn't been mentioned at our squad meeting that morning. Frankly, we had to be professional and cut off from it. That was our job. That's what the public has a right to expect of us, how ever angry and yet powerless we may have felt.

The journey to the stadium – the Marseilles Vélodrome – was assisted by a magnificent police escort of ten motor-cycles and numerous cars, not to mention the helicopter overhead. It would be hard to get used to London traffic after this! In Marseilles, there was far less traffic than I'd expected. Or maybe they deliberately took us on a route they knew would be quieter. Whatever, it was very well organized and again made us realize the size of the event.

Our journey lasted some forty minutes. Gary Guyan had put together three videos to lift the players during the drive. One of the tapes was the same one we'd run in Rome; the others were longer, and featured recent goals we'd scored mixed with action from training sessions, all cut to the track that had first rung out on that memorable night in Rome. 'Search For The Hero Inside Yourself' was becoming something of a theme tune. As I had hoped, the videos provided a good focus. I'd had one eye on them, not taking too much in, when suddenly the number of fans outside started to grow and I realized that we were almost upon the stadium. The reaction of the fans the closer we got to the Vélodrome was fantastic, and the players were visibly lifted. There was a feeling of anticipation on the coach, but also tension – I felt none. Normally, I get a bit of a tingle and a few butterflies in my tummy, particularly when I see the fans. But before this game I was completely relaxed.

The first thing we did was go out on to the pitch and soak up some of the atmosphere. It was everything we could have hoped for and more. Even though England, officially, had only 7,000 tickets, there must have been at least 20,000 England supporters inside. And they were in full voice. It was a far cry from the days when I played there with Monaco and things were thrown at us as we got off the bus. In those days we had to rush to the dressing room because the supporters were so frightening.

The playing surface was hard and very dry, and because the sun was so strong we spent some time working out whether David Seaman might need added protection, and whether there was an advantage to be gained from choosing to shoot towards a particular end should we win the toss. In football at this level you have to think of all sorts of things; you're always looking for little advantages. Actually, there wasn't any advantage to be gained from the sun so I told Alan and the players that I thought we ought to kick into the end where the bulk of our fans were. I'd always had this hunch that if we got our noses ahead, Tunisia would find it hard to come back.

Before kick-off, I made sure I had a word with all twenty-two players. Nerves weren't showing but determination was. I noticed particularly that Paul Scholes, of whom so much was expected in what people like to describe as the 'play-maker's' role, didn't seem phased by the occasion. I pulled every one of the substitutes aside one by one and reminded them how important it was to make good use of their time on the bench. I said to Michael Owen, 'Watch the defenders. Work out which are their stronger sides; who's big and cumbersome, who's small and nippy. If I send you on, you've got to be ready.' John came back from warming up with the players to report that they all looked really up for it.

Paul Ince does his own warm-up in the dressing room. It works for him. It is what he has always done. And it gave me the ideal opportunity to have a good long chat with him and remind him how important it was that he didn't get himself booked for something silly. I'd always planned to do it then; the longer I left it, the fresher it would be in his mind. How would you feel, I asked him, if we reached the semi-final and you couldn't play because you'd been back-chatting to the referee in an earlier game? It certainly made him think. I also told him that if he and David Batty dictated things and won the ball off the Tunisians in the middle of the park then we would be able to win from there.

As it turned out, there was just one moment in the second half when Incey got involved in a fracas with the Tunisian bench. I immediately jumped up and pointed at him, and the penny must have dropped because he cooled down pretty quickly after that.

My outstanding memory from the match was our first goal – Alan Shearer's header. I remember going to stand in the zone in front of our bench to shout out some instructions – only the coach was allowed to do that – and while I was out there we got a free-kick out on the right. Immediately, I sensed that this could be our moment; I really fancied us from set-plays. I was going to stay standing but instead, I crouched down so that everyone behind me could see, and as I crouched down, we did the two dummy runs, the signal went up … and bang, the ball was in the back of the net. Brilliant. It was a wonderful feeling to turn round and see everyone on the bench celebrating.

Of course, as a coach you move very quickly from feeling elated to realizing that you have to calm everyone down and make sure the players concentrate. It's the old cliché: you're never more vulnerable than when you've just scored. Of course Alan enjoyed the goal, the players enjoyed it, we all enjoyed it, but we needed to react professionally and make sure we didn't concede a goal in those vulnerable couple of minutes immediately afterwards. We'd had a scare early on – a deflected shot that could have gone anywhere, including past David Seaman, after the defence was caught out for about the only time. That moment aside, the best chances were ours. Eventually, minutes from the end, Paul Scholes, who'd had a couple of them, scored our second with a wonderful shot that curled round the keeper. I was delighted with the way Incey went past the two players to set Scholesy up; had Incey lost the ball the Tunisians would have been able to counter-attack and Ince would have been out of position as our deepest lying midfielder. It was a fine line between us scoring and them breaking. When the ball reached Scholesy I knew he was going to shoot but I didn't expect him to get such a good whip on the ball. That second goal was decisive. I felt really pleased for Scholesy, a quiet lad who doesn't like the limelight, but who will have to get used to it.

It was the perfect climax to our afternoon in the heat of Marseilles. It had been crucial to get off to a winning start.

And we'd done it. Our dressing room was a wonderfully happy place to be. All of us had known that anything other than a victory in the first game would have put us under great pressure. Ask the Spanish – they had lost their first game, and could be in trouble.

I was particularly pleased with the manner of the victory, and with individual performances. Playing David Batty and Paul Ince together in the middle of the park to control the game worked well. The Tunisians never broke that control despite the fact that they've got some good offensive players. We knew they couldn't finish. In fact, I'd warned our players against bringing anyone down in a one-on-one situation because the chances were they wouldn't have scored anyway. They had no conviction up front. In fact, they didn't really create a decent chance after the first few minutes apart from a couple of long distance shots.

After the game we had to wait a long time for Teddy Sheringham and Gareth Southgate, who had been randomly chosen for drug testing. Two players from each team always are. It was hot and they were obviously dehydrated, hence the long delay. While we were waiting, I watched our next opponents Romania play Colombia on TV in the office of the stadium director, who I remembered from my playing days in France. He was extremely friendly, although I'm sure he was finding out how good my French was. He wouldn't have been impressed! It was a bonus to catch the game, although Peter Taylor and Dave Sexton were in Lyon anyway, compiling reports on both teams to help our preparation.

The coach taking us back to Marseilles airport for the flight to San Nazaire seemed to take an age, despite the escort. We made up some time at the airport, however, since we were driven straight on to the tarmac and given preference for take-off, which apparently peeved our family and friends no end! We knew, from phone calls that were made after the match, that they were already at the airport, and as we were waiting to take off we were convinced we could see them about to board their plane back to Luton. I started waving frantically to someone who looked remarkably like Vanessa, but after a short time I wasn't so sure! Embarrassingly, the plane turned out to be a scheduled flight to Paris ... but it didn't stop the passengers waving back. Would you believe that the woman I waved to even sent me a fax two days later? What she said will remain a secret. I can see the headline now: 'Hoddle Waves To Mystery Woman Shock!' The mood, once we got airborne ourselves, was remarkably contented, but not noisy or exuberant. We were one game down with six to go, hopefully.

Back at La Baule, the locals lined the streets to welcome us 'home'. La Baule is only a small village and the reception we got initially had been very low key but warm. From what I can gather, the French commentators had really talked up our performance against Tunisia though and the local people were starting to get World Cup fever. It was a good feeling.

Some of the players, staff and I bolted down our dinner in time to watch the Germans play the USA. The Germans won, predictably, but they weren't particularly convincing. I didn't think we would have anything to fear if we met them later in the tournament. We could look forward to that with confidence. The Americans looked very ordinary. I knew they'd struggle to get anything out of their group.

The staff, including myself, had a few drinks before turning in, but there was no alcohol for the players, nor would there be until at least two days after the game. It's the last thing the body needs when it's dehydrated, when there's lactic acid building up in the muscles. I know that when I was a player we would have had a few drinks on the plane after winning our first World Cup match, and a few more back at the hotel, too. In 1990 – and probably in 1996, too – there was too much alcohol consumed after a game. But my players knew the score, and not one of them asked for a drink. They knew that they had to make sacrifices, and they understood why.

It took me a moment or two to work out that night that we had been in France for almost a week. The days had been so full that I had lost track of time and had to keep asking people what day it was. I was living my life according to 'match day'. But as I settled down to sleep that night, I was very sure about where we were at: we had just won the first match of our World Cup campaign and could look forward with confidence to our next one, against Romania, a week later. I felt really happy and contented. I'd spoken to a few people back home – the kids, Anne, my mum and dad – and they were all thrilled for me and for everybody. It was a lovely feeling. As I drifted off, I said a quick prayer – of thanks.

CHAPTER 8

WINNING
PROBLEMS

16 – 21 JUNE 1998

The morning after a winning start to the World Cup campaign, we were up early. On the golf course. Staff only. Everybody was on a high after the result against Tunisia and we had a lot of laughs. I was still thrilled about how well all the staff got on with each other; there was a real feeling that we were all in it together. Mind you, the rivalry on the golf course was as intense as ever, and I enjoyed giving Clem a thrashing and coming out £100 up on the day.

We had left the players to sleep in – the previous day had been a long one – and we only had a light training session that afternoon, just stretching for those that had played. John and I took a practice match for those that hadn't; it was vitally important to keep their spirits up. They responded fantastically, with 250 local children wearing England T-shirts cheering them on. The kids, who regularly burst into applause during the session, got soft drinks and something to eat at our media centre before being presented with a bag of souvenirs. The mood at L'Escoublac was upbeat, and so it should have been, despite the fact that the press continued to highlight Becks and his disappointment at missing out on our opening game. But I'd had a long chat with David. He seemed OK. He said he understood. Besides, I had picked a team to win the match, and we had done so. Darren Anderton proved his fitness and it all worked out very well. End of story. At least it should have been.

Back at the hotel, with yet another press conference coming up, we decided to have a go at the *Sunday People* which, twenty-four hours before the Tunisia match, had splashed David Seaman's private life across its front page. It was exactly what I'd asked the editors not to do back at Stoke Poges during our golf day in May. I said what I thought about it on live television, which is the one advantage that twenty-four-hours-a-day, seven-days-a-week news channels give us. We were fighting our corner. The story really annoyed me. If it had to be run, it could have appeared at any time. I could see it upset David too, although being the experienced campaigner he is, he didn't let it affect his performance. He thanked me later for our support. I'll stick by any of the players under similar circumstances.

Mind you, that wasn't the only incident which had affected my good mood that Tuesday. I had been told, just as I was heading over to talk to the press, that Gareth Southgate had jarred his ankle. I thought things were going too well – I was so furious I had to stop on the way over to calm down. It was a freak accident – he went over on his ankle trying to retrieve a pass from David Batty – and his ankle was swollen and bruised. I thought he'd been overdoing things considering it was the day after a match. Gareth was very upset and I was fuming. There hadn't been many things that had got me really irritated during our trip so far, but this was one of them. I suspected that he'd torn his ankle ligaments, and it seemed such a trivial way to put a player out of a World Cup.

Wisely, most people kept their distance for a while – David Davies was with me and just let me simmer down. However, with time to reflect I realized that it could, in fact, help answer a problem for us. We had been considering tinkering with the line-up for the Romania game and playing Gary Neville because I felt he would give us the greater width we needed if we had to revert to a back four during the game. The idea that there might have been a reason for the injury improved my mood slightly.

That afternoon we watched Scotland get a 1–1 draw with Norway. I thought it was a great result as I fancied Norway to do well in France. Scotland would have been out had they lost. When they went 1–0 down I knew exactly what was going through Craig Brown's mind. He would have been debating whether to make a substitution, and if so, who to take off? Of course, his decision was made for him by Colin Calderwood's injury, and it was substitute Michael Weir's pass that set up Craig Burley's goal. I was pleased for Burley, who played for me at Chelsea. He played well.

Everyone in our camp was up for that game, watching it together in the video room on the big screen. Our bookies had taken a packet and I was down on about ten different bets. I hadn't had one sniff. But as I went for a 1–1 draw I cleared the decks – it was unusual because I'm the world's worst at predicting results. Alan and Teddy took their roles as resident bookies very seriously; it was entertaining listening to them carry on. It seemed as though they were more concerned with the identity of the first goalscorer than with the game itself. The banter that goes on was entertainment in itself.

I'm sure there were a few flutters on Ronaldo notching his first goal of the Finals that night against Morocco, too. He duly obliged, and a group of us, players and staff, were lucky enough to be inside the stadium in Nantes to witness it. Morocco had impressed in their first game against Norway but they seemed just glad to be there on this occasion, as I was; it gave me the chance to switch off a bit, although I still made a few notes – just in case.

It struck me, watching Brazil that night, what a special occasion it was. Of course, the team's got wonderful flair, but when Brazil play, it's far more than just a game; it's an event. There's an aura about Brazil that captivates neutrals, which is why ten of our players went to watch the game as well. Not everyone, however, wanted to come. When Michelle Farrer asked who was up for it, Gareth Southgate said, 'Why should we go? They wouldn't come and see us, would they?' That's the other view. When you play them you have to shut off from the aura that surrounds them. They're not arrogant, but they do believe they are the best.

However, I felt that winning the World Cup might be beyond them on this occasion. I fancied someone could topple them at some time over seven games – their style of play was so open. And although Dunga has been a terrific player he was still the one expected to fill in at the back even though his legs were going. I certainly saw enough during the game to suggest that we could have created chances against them.

I saw Michel Platini, who I don't know well, at half-time, and told him how sorry I was for the terrible death of his friend and colleague Mr Sastre. Michel Platini still looked as if he was grieving. I also told him that he ought to be proud of the way the tournament was going. He just looked at me and said, 'It's going to be interesting. Who's going to win it? It's very open.' I said I thought there were lots of teams that could win it, and he just said, 'Maybe you, eh?' in such a way that made me think he was really convinced we were in with a shout. I walked back to my seat feeling good after that.

Mind you, I didn't need Platini to tell me what a great chance we had. I knew it myself, and nothing I had seen since the start of the tournament had made me think otherwise. At that stage, I felt it would be a big shock to my system if we didn't win the World Cup.

But I wasn't going to broadcast that fact to the media, as Alan Shearer inadvertently had done during one of our press conferences. I'd told the players that we should act like world champions because we were going to be world champions. 'The gaffer's told us we're going to win it,' Alan had said. I had said that but Alan had forgotten that I didn't want it made public. Luckily, it didn't turn into a headline. It would have meant more pressure.

Three events over the course of the two days following the Tunisia game put what we were doing into perspective. Firstly, on the Tuesday my cousin Michelle gave birth to her first baby. She'd had a hard time in delivery but both she and the baby – a boy called Deon – were doing fine. I phoned her in the hospital and she burst into tears as soon as she heard my voice, which got me really upset. We were both congratulating each other. She's very special to me; I've been babysitting her since she was four years old.

Then on the Wednesday, in La Baule, we were represented at a British military cemetery where fifty Second World War veterans – English and French – were commemorating a terrible incident in 1940 in which more – possibly many more – than 3,000 British soldiers died when their ship was bombed by the Germans in the nearby estuary. The Lancastria went down in less than fifteen minutes. So many young men – the same ages as our players – were killed as 500 tons of oil spilled into the sea.

Thirdly, just before Wednesday's training session, David Beckham made a special phone call to a young boy back home who was in a coma after two heart attacks. Alex, a Manchester United fan, was suffering from the same disease that killed Terry Yorath's son, and his family and friends thought there was a chance he might react to a message from his hero if it was played to him. They wanted to include

David's message in videos and recordings of recent England and United games to try to bring him back.

While David was making his phone call, we received one – from the editor of the *Sunday People*, Neil Wallis, who was upset at our public complaint about his paper running a story about David Seaman the day before a match. According to him the whole thing had been David's fault! No mention of who decides what goes in his paper. No mention of the potential upset to a player who is key to a team his paper claims to be backing. It wasn't a football matter. Assuming the paper was backing us, my question had to be, 'Was that story helpful?'

Thankfully, I had a chance to let off some steam when the coaching and medical staff staged a five-a-side replay of the game we first played back in Rome. Rob Lee recorded it on video it for us, and it was a hell of a game. The coaching staff won 5-4; we were winding them up in the end. Glenn Roeder scored two, as did Peter Taylor, and I scored a peach of a goal after just thirty seconds. Our keeper (and security chief), Ray Whitworth, had picked up a back pass and the Doc, who was refereeing, waved play on. As you can imagine, there was mayhem. It took five minutes to sort it out and while everyone was arguing I noticed their keeper, Gary Lewin, off his line. So I grabbed the ball, said, 'It must be our free-kick then, Doc,' and spun it over Gary's head. It hit the underside of the bar and went in. We were all claiming 1–0 and the Doc didn't know what to do! Then Clem, who wouldn't play in goal because he can't kick from there any more, brought Brian Scott down and Glenn Roeder booted the ball at him, all in good fun – and it all went off. There would have been a few red cards under the FIFA rules. But the Doc had forgotten them!

Would a game against the press be played in a similar spirit? They were all still keen, I knew, because Lee Clayton of the *Daily Star* had asked us about it again. I wanted it to happen, but there didn't seem to be a right time. Perhaps we could demand the right to pick their team! It wouldn't take us long to choose the usual suspects. Whether they'd all turn out was a different matter! David Davies wanted to insist that we selected their team.

David, incidentally, flew home that night for twenty-four hours. His daughter, Caroline, had been told she needed an operation on her spine, and with his mother ill as well, I knew that he was very worried about how his wife would cope. These are the human problems behind every team effort.

On Thursday, our tenth day in La Baule, I gave everyone the day off, which as usual was the signal for a golf tournament in the morning, although some of the players went shopping and had a bit of fun on the beach. It was a restful day, hassle-free. To top it off we all went out for dinner in the evening to a restaurant that we had earmarked back in April when we'd done that recce in La Baule. The restaurant was designed to resemble a boat and we took over the entire top deck. It was a great night. The laughs got louder and louder as the evening wore on and the games got more and more rowdy. I'm still reminding John that he promised to give £100 to anyone who could do a press-up with straight arms. It's ever so hard; I've only ever seen John do it. But Terry Byrne got up and did it easily, at which point the boys creased up. John still hasn't paid up, but then he is Scottish!

We got back to the hotel in time to catch the second half of the match between France and South Africa, and to see Zidane sent off. That meant we'd suddenly seen five sendings-off in tournament games, which was a bit worrying. Despite all the pre-tournament fears surrounding the new FIFA rules it had all started so well, but I think the referees went a bit too far the other way after Platini and Sepp Blatter claimed they weren't being strict enough in their interpretation of tackles from behind. It was a shame, because we wanted to see eleven play eleven in this World Cup.

As if I hadn't laughed enough during our meal out the previous night, a report on Sky News the following morning had me in fits of laughter again. They'd painstakingly filmed all the good bits of La Baule that the England players, they claimed, were missing out on because of their strict regime and rigid diet: the beach (which is among the best in Europe) and the good restaurants – yet all the time we were sitting in one of those restaurants, 500 yards up the road, enjoying some great fish and a couple of glasses of wine each, with our World Cup coach parked large as life outside. I know how difficult it must be to fill twenty-four hours of airtime, but that was ridiculous.

So was the baked bean saga – built up after one of many articles about our excellent chef, Roger. We only took baked beans off the menu on match days (because they are hard to digest) but this became 'England Ban Beans'. Hilarious! As I said to the coaching staff, if 'the great baked bean controversy' was the only thing we had to worry about then we didn't have a problem. Incidentally, there was no ban on milk either, as some reported. Surely the major issue was whether we won the games or not? Some of the minor issues that the press focused on made me laugh, but didn't do much to change my opinion of what matters to some journalists.

Before our training session on the Friday morning we showed the players some clips from the game against Tunisia that highlighted the parts of our game I felt we still needed to work on. We also ran a couple of videos of Romania in action; with four days to go until the game it was time to focus totally on the task that lay ahead of us.

Fortunately, three of the four players who had missed training on Wednesday – Alan Shearer, Teddy Sheringham and Tony Adams – were back in full training. Tony and Alan had decided to wear studs in Marseilles despite the rock-hard pitch; looking back they should have worn rubbers like the others. Tony inflamed a tendon underneath his foot, and Alan's feet were pretty raw, too. But neither injury was serious. Teddy had been the biggest worry. Doc Crane and John Gorman had appeared, looking glum, at my door to report a possible hamstring problem that fortunately turned out to be nothing more than a build-up of lactic acid in Teddy's muscles. But I had already accepted that Gareth Southgate's ankle problem wasn't going to clear up in time for Monday's game, which would give Gary Neville his chance.

I didn't name the team until just before we left the hotel to train the following morning. Gary Neville's inclusion apart, there was nothing unusual about the team – except that it was the first time I'd ever named a team in pitch darkness! I didn't mean to. We'd been watching another forty-five-minute video of Romania. Gary Guyan had recorded all their set-plays back-to-back and added in excerpts from their match against Colombia, so it was bang up to date. The lights, of course, had been dimmed for the video, and were still down when I named the team. I didn't even realize how dark it was at the time but afterwards I said to John, 'That's a new one. I named the team and I couldn't see a bloody player!'

Still, there was only the one change. But I was determined not to make the change public, and our training session was closed to the press until the last twenty minutes. There were no obvious clues as to who was in and who was out when the cameras were admitted. Our aim was to keep the Romanian coach guessing rather than the press. We had a source trying to find out the injury situation within the Romanian camp and I'm sure they were up to the same tricks. It goes on all the time in big games. I never considered Tunisia to be a major problem, but for the Romanian match we were certainly going to pretend that Gareth was fit when he wasn't. I had no qualms about it; I was just doing my job as a coach. Gary Neville and Gareth Southgate are physically different:

Gareth's stronger in the air (although Gary's got other attributes) which meant that the opposition would have to alter their game plan, particularly in terms of set-plays. That might not be obvious to everyone, but every coach would know where I was coming from.

Gareth was very honest to me about his injury but his disappointment was obvious. The press wanted to talk to him, and I didn't want to block it. I told him and all the players to stick to the line that the team hadn't been named and that Gareth was making progress (which he was). Let's be clear – the Romanians would have been delighted to be told in advance that Gareth wasn't playing.

Aside from that straight swap, I wasn't tempted to change the line-up one bit, despite the public clamour for Michael Owen and David Beckham to start. I hadn't changed my opinion that Becks hadn't been focused for the start of the tournament and was only just getting back on track; as for Michael, he was earmarked for the third game even before we arrived in France. I always had him in mind for Colombia because they were playing very flat and square at the back, which would suit Michael's game perfectly. He still has a lot to learn about getting off the hook of man-to-man marking and evading a deep-lying sweeper – which both Tunisia and Romania were using – and finding space to receive the ball. Both Alan and Teddy have experience of that, and Romania was a game that cried out for experienced players.

Spirits were high in the camp, even though the press were claiming that Becks was still very down (despite the fact that he was training as hard as anyone). The biggest laugh of that Saturday was provided by the Doc on the coach, who was covered in sun cream that wouldn't rub in properly. He looked like a ghost! Or at least he did after Clem put some more on him. It was a baking hot day and we made sure all the players and staff were well protected. But the Doc took it a bit too far. The cream was everywhere – in his hair, his eyes, up his nose. It took him hours to get it all out. He's a good doctor and a fantastic character, a great raconteur who we were going to miss after the World Cup. That's why I asked him to stay on as a consultant, so hopefully this tournament won't prove to have been his swan song.

Despite the scorching heat, the game between Japan and Croatia at Nantes that afternoon was a really open one. It was the second match I'd seen, and once again the atmosphere was marvellous. It doesn't come across on television; you just have to be there. I had a good long look at Croatia, who we knew could be our opponents in the last sixteen. Although they beat the Japanese with a goal from Davor Suker I felt confident we could find a way past them.

Actually, I had a bet on the Japanese beforehand, as the odds from our bookies were too tempting. In keeping with the rest of my bets during this World Cup, however, it went down the pan. By this time, though, our bookies were not quite as cocky as they had been at the start of the tournament. A couple of heavy losses had clipped their wings. Sadly it was nothing whatsoever to do with me!

After dinner that night I sat outside talking to the other coaches. The weather at last was hot and dry, totally different to the wet weather of a week earlier, and it was a lovely way to chill out. Everyone was telling jokes and getting involved in wind-ups, and there were little innuendoes flying around. There were some great characters in the camp, right through from the kitman, Martin Grogan, to Peter Taylor and John, both of whom have the gift of the gab. We were all kicking the same way.

Later, as we watched Holland wallop South Korea 5–0, I wondered aloud whether we would come up against the Dutch at some stage. They looked a good side with a great system, and had to be one of the tournament favourites. It would have been a totally different proposition, of course, to when we beat them during Euro '96. We'd be playing on a neutral ground, for starters and they were a better side than they were two years ago. But so were we. I would have loved the challenge.

Wagons rolled on Sunday afternoon as we left for Toulouse, where we were to face Romania (who were the seeded team in our group and the favourites, as I reminded the press) that night. The only noteworthy moment during the forty-five-minute journey came when the pilot informed us that the Germans, who had been losing 2–0 to Yugoslavia in their group match before we left La Baule, had pulled the score back to 2–2. It wasn't much of a surprise; they were still the team to beat. But while the news brought groans all around me on the plane, I have to admit that I was quite pleased. I wanted the Germans to top their group and for us to see them off in the quarter-finals. We had a score or two to settle.

As we landed we could see our security adviser, Sir Brian Hayes, standing on the tarmac. He'd had a rough few days thanks to the *Daily Mirror*, which had accused him of shirking his responsibilities because he had spent the last few days in Spain on family business. Needless to say, the lads – led by their captain – needed no encouragement to have a wind-up with him. Alan came straight out with the line, 'Like the suntan, Sir Brian. Had a nice break?' Sir Brian smiled through gritted teeth but gave as good as he got. 'Can you play with a broken leg tomorrow?' he asked Alan, which had the whole coach doubled up in laughter. I don't suppose there were too many in Sir Brian's last job at Scotland Yard who talked to him like Alan did!

But he had every right to be angry about the *Daily Mirror* stories. Our security continued to be very tight on our travels. With the French version of the SAS with us, we did wonder what drama they were expecting – particularly when they all piled out of the car that travelled in front of our coach within seconds of us stopping, rifles at the ready.

Meanwhile, Paul Scholes also suffered at the hands of the *Mirror*, which published pictures of his new home. The pictures seemed to have been taken on his property without permission. There was also an interview with his girlfriend that was just made up in another paper! Paul was really upset and rightly so.

That afternoon in Toulouse we trained at the Municipale Stadium, which, they say, is known as the Little Wembley. It promised a Wembley-like atmosphere, that's for sure. But I was concerned about two things: how dry the grass was – we needed it well watered for the game – and the fact that the media were allowed to congregate along the touchline. They were there en masse by the time we arrived and could actually hear what we were saying to one another. I was much happier down in Marseilles where they were behind one goal or in the stand. It was something I needed to sort out for the future.

The press had plenty to occupy them. They were particularly interested in the fitness of Gareth Southgate, who found a camera up his nose wherever he turned; and the fact that Alex Ferguson had chosen the day before a crucial World Cup match to go public on Becks, and how I'd treated him. It's exactly the sort of thing Alex would go so ballistic about, if he was on the receiving end of criticism from me on the eve of a Champions' League match.

Of course, the press wanted me to respond and make the next day's headlines for them, but there was no way I was going to give them what they wanted, not until after the match. I had to give them ten out of ten for effort, though: they tried six times during the mixed-zone press conference that followed our training session to get me to play ball. I told them I'd got far more important things to deal with, which was true. But I was furious inside.

As soon as Alex's comments in the *Sunday Times* were shown to me, I knew that the press would try and get me to hit back, and I had a choice to make. It wasn't a difficult one. I could see the headlines the next morning if I did what they wanted, headlines that would send out the wrong signal to the nation on the day of such a crucial World Cup game. That was the last thing I wanted. I wanted to talk about the game, about Romania and England, about what it meant and about how tough it was going to be. So I wouldn't budge.

Deep down, I was dreadfully disappointed with Alex. It was crazy of him to come out and say what he did the day before such a big game, however strongly he felt. I can't tell you how many times the press have asked me for quotes on United's chances the day before one of their big European ties, and how many times I've declined because I didn't think it would be fair to Alex or to his players. Of course he's entitled to his opinions – everyone is – but surely he could have picked up the phone first and talked to me. His response was wrong, and gave us a headache we could have done without. He must have known that, with all his experience.

The problem was that Alex was furious that I had allowed David to talk to the press after he'd been left out of the team for Tunisia. Alex believed David was still suffering and should have been shielded from the media's attention. In fact he did that press conference more than four days after he'd been told that he wasn't in the starting line-up. We were in a tournament situation. David was part of the squad. Imagine the headlines if David had been prevented from speaking to anyone for days on end. I wanted him to make clear he understood the decision, say that he was disappointed but that he was ready and willing when called upon.

If the press had a field day it was because when David is upset, it shows. But I was convinced he would learn from the situation when he had had a chance to take it all in. I'm sure he went back into his room after I'd told him he was dropped and said to his room-mate Gary Neville, 'I can't believe he's done this.' But deep down I think he understood my reasons, and I think what I did gave him a big jolt, made him realize that the World Cup had to come before everything else in his life. Fine, he's in love, but I think he lost his way a bit at the end of last season and his form suffered as a result. Don't get me wrong: David's a marvellous player and I love him dearly. Had he been focused I would certainly have played him and kept Darren back. But he wasn't.

Back at the hotel that night the bookies got a hammering when Iran beat the USA 2–1. You could hear the cheering all over the hotel as we were having a nightcap in the bar afterwards. CNN did a feature on the game saying that the whole country was out on the streets celebrating the victory.

I seemed to be the only person in the camp who didn't benefit from the bookies that night. I didn't bother with a bet; I never do the night before a game. By that time it's only England's results that matter to me.

CHAPTER 9

ROMANIA–A BAD FEELING

22 JUNE 1998

O ur mid-morning training session on Monday 22 June, at a small stadium about fifteen minutes from our Toulouse hotel, was supposed to be a secret. But you would never have guessed it from the number of villagers – not to mention about 200 local policemen – who had got wind of our arrival and turned out to greet us. I'd never seen anything like it – they lined the road for at least a mile. It gave the players a lift, but I was the most concerned person around.

I'd woken up that morning with a very bad feeling. I couldn't explain it. But it was there. I knew Romania were a quality side; they weren't the seeded team in our group for nothing. But I just couldn't shake the feeling off. It stayed with me right up until kick-off at 9 p.m. and throughout the entire game.

However, there was no way I was going to let it affect our final preparations. We still had some work to do on the training ground: we needed to put the finishing touches to some set-plays and run through some tactics. In particular, I wanted to make sure that the players knew in which areas of the pitch they had to close the Romanians down to prevent them playing their passing game.

It was a good session and a vital one too, but we walked the players through it really. There was absolutely no point in exerting them too hard so close to such a crucial game. We'd already talked about how we thought Romania would shape up, and in particular about the threat the veteran Hagi might pose. I knew we probably wouldn't see him do much defending, that he would probably hang upfield in an area where he could hurt us if he got the ball and we weren't pre-pared. Sol Campbell was the key man in this respect. I told Sol that if Hagi got the ball in the last third of the pitch he would have to close him down as early as possible.

The last part of the session was very light, really just for fun and to make sure everyone was relaxed. The players seemed to have taken everything on board and the mood was positive. But I still had this strange feeling. I felt happy with the work we'd done. I felt happy with the team I'd selected. I was still sure that we were going to qualify from our group and make progress from there. Nevertheless, the feeling I had deep down about the game with Romania was not the feeling I'd had before our qualifying games in Rome and in Poland when I'd just known we were going to succeed. This time, I had the opposite feeling, that we weren't going to win. Call it a gut feeling, call it whatever you want – I couldn't shake it off, how ever much I tried.

The last time I'd had such a sense of foreboding was in the coach on the way to face Chile at Wembley. I told John that I didn't feel good about that match, and sure enough we lost 2–0. But although that game did have some value as a World Cup warm-up, it was still only a friendly. This game against Romania was a totally different proposition altogether, and it was desperately unsettling to feel the way I did.

Colombia didn't help my cause by snatching a winner against Tunisia in the other Group G game being played that afternoon. It had kicked off at 5.30 p.m. while we were still finishing our pre-match meal – poached eggs, yoghurt, tea and toast – so we missed the first ten minutes. We also missed the last ten as we had to leave for our game in Toulouse, but we caught the majority of it on the hotel's massive screen. I've never seen anything like it in any hotel, anywhere. It was like a cinema screen. There were at least 400 people watching.

I thought Tunisia were superb in the first half. They should have wrapped the match up with the amount of chances they had, and I wish they had; a Tunisian win, or even a draw, would have suited us. But of course, as we boarded our coach for Toulouse's Municipale stadium, French radio told us the news that we didn't want to hear – that Colombia had scored. It was another bad sign and just added to my feeling that it wasn't going to be our day.

However, I couldn't afford to let it get me down. We still had our job ahead of us; all we could do was try our best to beat Romania and put ourselves on the top of Group G.

The journey to any game is always a strange time for a coach. In a sense, it's out of your hands from then on. You've done all you can to prepare the players for the game, except the pre-match pep talks in the dressing room. And once there, I said all the right things. Our preparation was no different to what it had always been: spot on. But as I sat on that bench during the game, half of me was still trying to shrug off the feeling that it just wasn't going to happen for us – so it wasn't a surprise to me when Romania went 1–0 up. Even when Michael Owen got us back on level terms I was still sitting uneasily on my seat. I did tell John I thought we could still win it, but I didn't have the same conviction that I'd had in Rome and in Poland.

When they scored again through my ex-Chelsea colleague Dan Petrescu of all people, it was an awful feeling but again, no surprise. Funnily enough, I still thought we might get a 2–2 draw, but although Michael Owen hit the post, it just wasn't to be our night.

However, I was happy with our performance, despite the defeat, and I'm convinced that had we got a 1–1 draw people would have said it was a good comeback, and that we should have won. I certainly wouldn't have done anything differently given the chance again. OK, so we didn't press them as hard as we'd pressed Tunisia when we got behind the ball. We thought we'd done our job by just dropping off them. It was something I addressed with the players at half-time. But generally our approach was right, the tactics were right, our shape was right. We had enough opportunities, and got in enough areas to punish the Romanians, but we didn't really pick out the right ball on the night. And although we didn't defend poorly apart from the goals, we went to sleep twice and paid the price. I can't justify somebody's touch not being good or somebody being a little bit out of form. The way we lost – by giving away two stupid goals – was very unlike us.

The first goal came about simply through lack of concentration on our part. We had spoken about pushing Hagi down the right and not letting him come inside on to his left foot. So when they got the throw-in on the right I was watching Graeme Le Saux. I said to John, 'Graeme's on the wrong side.' Of course the ball came inside to Hagi, who hooked it into the penalty area where Tony's position was wrong as well. As soon as Moldovan took the ball on his chest I thought, that's it. It was galling to get caught out from a dead-ball situation after all the work we'd put in to prevent that happening. It would have been slightly easier to take if they had created a magnificent goal.

Of course, it hadn't helped that we had lost Incey twenty minutes into the game with an ankle injury, even though

David Beckham came on and did very well. He got himself into the game very quickly. I'd told him not to be afraid to go out wide and get Darren to fill in for him inside, and in the second half they started to rotate just as I'd always envisaged. I saw TV pictures afterwards of John and I frantically going through the notes we had made on set-plays with Becks while he was tying his laces ready to go on. Incey was an important player to us on set-plays, particularly defensively, and we had to readjust because David doesn't have Incey's natural defensive qualities. Some people might question the wisdom of asking a player to take instructions on board in the heat of the moment, but if I had failed to tell him and we had lost a goal because of it, I wouldn't be doing my job as coach properly. I've always maintained that the knowledge you give players is one thing; remembering it when you need it is another – especially when there are 40,000 people watching you.

Overall the atmosphere at the stadium was marvellous. But I find it interesting – if occasionally frustrating – to hear the supporters sitting within earshot of the bench change their attitude so dramatically. A minute before we got our goal a fan just behind us was effing and blinding for all he was worth. 'I paid £200 for this seat,' he was shouting. '£200 to watch this load of crap.' A minute later the same guy was roaring us on. 'We're going to win, well done lads,' he was crowing. John and I just looked at each other. You get used to that sort of thing.

Of course I could hear the fans chanting for me to bring Michael on – how could I not hear 20,000-odd people in full voice – but it made no difference whatsoever to my game plan. A coach has to be more professional than that. Sitting on that bench after we went 1–0 down I was mulling things over in my mind – shall I change this, shall I change that? I was always sure that young Michael was going to play a part at some stage. We had nursed him into this World Cup and I felt it was right to put him on when I did, with twenty-five minutes to go. And so it proved. He got the goal and he hit the post as well.

So I was really annoyed with Kevin Keegan's comments. I watched the game later on and heard him say, 'Well, that's fan power for you'. when Michael and David Beckham came on. Absolute rubbish. At the very top level you make your own decisions for the right reasons and live by them.

Instead of looking at it positively and saying, 'Well he went on and scored so the timing was right,' people have criticized me for not bringing Michael on earlier. I brought Michael on when I did because I felt Teddy wasn't playing particularly well at the time. I don't believe in change for change's sake. It might be forced upon you by a change the opposition has made, or simply because one of your players is off-form, which is what happened in this case. We could have taken Scholesy off and put Michael up front alongside Alan, with Teddy playing just off them, but Teddy just wasn't on his game. Mind you, we'd had Michael warming up for ten minutes before he went on, so Teddy did have the chance to earn a reprieve. I've learnt from experience that you have to be flexible when it comes to substitutions. I remember in my second game in charge at Swindon – Plymouth away – our No. 8, Duncan Shearer, was having a nightmare so I told John to get him off. But just as we were about to substitute him – bang, he scored. He scored a hat-trick in the last twenty minutes! It was an early lesson in my apprenticeship as a manager.

The immediate aftermath of the game was very frustrating. All you want to do – win or lose – is get into the dressing room with the players but you have to do the usual 'flash interviews', which I still find a pain in the neck. While I was doing them I saw the second Romanian goal on the monitor. It was a terrible goal to give away, and I went straight into the dressing room and told the players so. I told them they couldn't defend like schoolboys at this level.

They were really down, naturally. Many of them sat silent and expressionless for a long time. It had been the cruellest way to lose. But I couldn't beat around the bush. I told them that there hadn't been much wrong with their performance; that they hadn't deserved to lose the game; that they'd worked hard enough to get a result; that they might have won it had their passing been more creative – but that they had thrown the game away with schoolboy defending. I told Graeme Le Saux that he should have been stronger, that come hell or high water he should have cleared that ball. I exchanged a few words with John and Ray Clemence, and Tony Adams too. Why had we lost concentration, I asked, and given away two such bad goals?

It was too soon for answers, and besides, I had to cut my words short because as usual I was under pressure to do the round of television, radio and press interviews. The pressure is even worse at World Cups because the TV stations have set satellite times for their interviews that must be kept to. But the good thing about the World Cup is that you've got the players for several days afterwards; under normal circumstances you've got about five minutes to say everything you need to because you won't see them again for weeks.

I told the players that we'd talk about the game, watch the video, and do whatever we had to do to put things right over the next few days. By that time, my voice was struggling (not for the first time after a game), and I was desperate for a hot drink. While Martin Grogan, our kit man, hunted for his kettle, I had to make do with a lukewarm cup of regulation FIFA coffee. FIFA's instructions were that coaches should get to their post-match press conferences within fifteen minutes of the final whistle. By the time we got to this one at least twenty minutes had elapsed since the end of the game. Was it surprising that I was in no hurry? When you lose at this level, whether you believe that you deserved to lose or not, you know what angle the media are going to take. You just have to face it. I did two TV interviews and then went into the mixed-zone press conference. I felt positive, I was honest, and I put my views across. Luckily the questions weren't particularly taxing.

The good news was that Ray Whitworth had managed to get the coaches containing our families into the car park which meant that we were able to see them for a short time. It gave everyone a much needed lift. In the dimly lit car park I embraced my mum, my brother Carl and Vanessa. There were a few tears. I was especially worried about my mum, who gets really wound up in key games. She takes it all very personally and had vowed never to go to a game after watching my second match as England coach, against Poland at Wembley. But she had come, and had turned white when the second Romanian goal went in. She turned so pale that Vanessa was worried that she was going to faint. She had obviously found it hard to cope with because she said to me, 'I'm not going to come again. It's not worth it.' At least at home she can dive into the kitchen or go out in the garden when the going gets tough.

It had been a worrying game for some of the other families, too. Many of them had found themselves in seats that were surrounded by the worst type of England fans: full of anger, hate and bad language. They weren't segregated at all and if there had been any trouble inside the ground they could have been in danger. I know how difficult it was to get tickets, but I think the families of players and staff deserved better.

After ten minutes or so, Ray was wandering around telling people it was time to go. The families had to catch their flight back to Luton. It was like a scene from visiting time in Ronnie Barker's *Porridge*. I felt sorry for Alan Shearer and Rob Lee, who saw their loved ones for less time than everybody else because they were delayed by the drugs tests.

Fortunately the wives and girlfriends would be returning for the Colombia game, and would be staying over on Friday night. By then we would hopefully have qualified for the last sixteen.

It was good to see everyone together, but I admit I was distant. I wanted to stay longer and talk, but inside I was so very disappointed (despite having feared the worst all day). At least everyone has been doing their best to make things work on the domestic front despite our problems. I'd been speaking to the children on a daily basis, and I'd spoken to Anne when I'd needed to. She had been very fair. Both she and Vanessa, understood the situation. Vanessa came out for the first two games, while Anne and the children were coming to the Colombia game. We've worked it out well.

My mum and dad were very supportive, too. They sent me a special card when we arrived in France that summed up everything that was going on in my life. It really touched me. It made me feel as if I was coping. But it didn't change the fact that whatever the difficulties at home, football had to be my priority.

It was about 1 a.m. by the time we reached Toulouse airport. The journey back – to our temporary 'home' of La Baule – took less than fifty minutes. There was a meal of lasagne and apple pie on offer, although some people, including our physio Alan Smith, opted out in favour of forty winks. I started talking to John and Clem about the consequences of the defeat. There was now a strong possibility that we would end up in the half of the draw that we hadn't expected. I couldn't really see Tunisia beating Romania, which would mean us finishing second in the group. Obviously we still had to get a draw or a win against Colombia, but if we got the right result it would mean a trip to St Etienne to meet either Argentina or Croatia.

Neither of them worried me greatly. But I could hardly start thinking about possible second round opponents before we had got past Colombia, even if my feelings about what had just happened very quickly turned from negative to positive. We had been beaten, but perhaps it was a good thing to have got the defeat out of our system. I was convinced that we could get back on track.

My mind was racing, but it was late. There was nothing to be gained from any more discussion that night. Eventually I said to John, 'Let's just switch off for a few hours if we can.' It helped. I remember that as we landed I was so overcome by a feeling of confidence that I looked over at Peter Taylor – who is invariably on the same wavelength as me – and started whistling 'Always Look on the Bright Side of Life'. Peter joined in and a few others started singing along. It just seemed the best thing to do. I'm aware that the players do sometimes look at me and wonder how I'm taking things; perhaps some of the staff do too (apart from John, Peter, Glenn and Ray, who know me so well). So I decided to lead from the front and try to relax everyone else as well.

Most of us were exhausted on arrival back in La Baule. It was past 3 a.m., and few bothered with the nightcap of soup and sandwiches that had been provided for us. The one piece of good news was that Incey's ankle injury, which had forced him out of the game early on, was not as bad as I had feared. I had a short chat with him and Sol Campbell before they went off to bed, which is when I heard the news that there had been some problems involving German fans in Lens and that a policeman was in a coma. I was shocked. When you hear that a tragedy like that has been indirectly caused by a game of football it puts everything into perspective.

However, apart from a few isolated incidents the World Cup had been marvellous up to this point. The football had been skilful and the atmosphere in the stadiums fantastic. Going into the tournament I felt it would be the hardest World Cup ever to win because the countries are so evenly matched these days, and that was the way it was panning

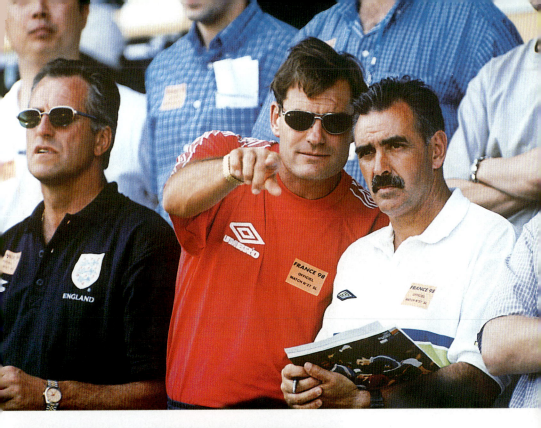

We enjoyed seeing our potential second round opponents in action when we watched Croatia beat Japan 1-0. I had always thought that Croatia could make a big impact on this World Cup tournament (above). Graeme Le Saux gets the better of Dan Petrescu during our second group match against Romania. Unfortunately the tables were turned at the end of the game when Petrescu snatched their winner.

(ALLSPORT, EMPICS)

David Beckham got his chance when he replaced Paul Ince (above) against Romania. Michael Owen came on for Teddy (below) and promptly scored a goal that brought us level (right). Issuing instructions during that match with Romania (below right). Only the coach was allowed to stand up in the area around the bench.

(COLORSPORT, EMPICS, ACTION PLUS)

The view that greeted our wives, girlfriends and families, in Lille, while they were travelling to Lens for our crunch match with Colombia (left). Inside the dressing room before the game (above and below left). The starting line-up for that crucial match – the winning team would go through, the loser would go home (below).

(Susan Davies, Tim Sonnex, Allsport)

David Beckham scored a great goal from this free-kick and we joined in the celebrations from the bench (left). Darren Anderton had already scored. It was a victory that took England through to the last sixteen (below).

(COLORSPORT, ACTION IMAGES, ALLSPORT)

At Chateau Tilques the squad enjoyed a light training session after our win. Later, we were forced to look for the nearest shelter – the luggage compartment of our coach – when we were caught in the driving rain as we said goodbye to our wives and girlfriends (above). With my co-author (right).

(SUSAN DAVIES, TIM SONNEX)

out. There had been goals galore, most of the games had been compulsive viewing and I thought it was the best World Cup there had been for many years.

I still felt that England could play a major part, as I told Michelle, David Davies and Brian Scott over a couple of beers before bed. It was late, but somehow I was reluctant to turn in. There was so much going on in my mind. But first and foremost, I knew that we all had to get over the disappointment of losing to Romania, and the manner of the defeat. It was a defeat we didn't expect but one we had to cope with. The fact was that as far as qualifying was concerned, the result made no difference. Win or lose, we would still have needed a point against Colombia on the Friday in a match that had now become do or die: winner to go through, loser to go home.

CHAPTER 10

COLOMBIA– BACK ON COURSE

23 – 26 JUNE 1998

People have different ways of dealing with losing – some go very quiet, others get loud and try to cover it up. Personally, I know that I have to deal with my emotions first before I can deal properly with anyone else's. As a coach you are always aware that your players are looking to you for guidance; how you respond is how they will eventually respond, too.

To clear my mind and focus my thoughts the morning after the Romanian defeat I had an early nine holes with some of the staff. It had the desired effect because I played well enough to take money off Ray again, this time on the last hole! The mood was pretty good, although Peter Taylor wasn't at the races. I had too much on my own plate to go into the whys and wherefores, but I could tell he just wasn't himself. However, it didn't stop us having a good game that put us in the right frame of mind to prepare for the day's training.

After lunch, we got all the players together out on the hotel's small training pitch. I gave it my best rallying cry. My aim was to try to reassure them that all was not lost, but also to make sure that they had learnt their lessons from the previous night's mistakes. I told them that the performance wasn't as bad as some people on television were trying to make out, but that we simply couldn't afford to make mistakes that would get punished. I reminded them that we had lost to Italy at Wembley during qualifying, but that I'd driven away from the stadium that night knowing that we'd still win our group, which we did. So it was vital that we remained positive. I also asked them the same question that I had asked them at Burnham Beeches before we left England: how do champions react to a loss? They draw on their self-belief and come back stronger than before, that's how.

Alan Shearer said a few things. He thought we hadn't created enough chances, that we had got into good positions without really pressurizing their goal. In the same vein I said that David Seaman wasn't exactly overworked, but that we had just fallen asleep twice. The players did respond a little bit more than usual but they were still very quiet. Morale was obviously low, but to be honest, I'd expected there to be a dip in the camp at this stage whether we had won or lost. We had been together for a long time; it was just human nature.

During training afterwards that dip in spirit was evident among the subs, and I had to address it with them. I sat them all down after the session and said, 'Look, I can only play eleven players at one given time, how ever much I would love to play you all. I've got to do what's right at the time. You might not agree with my decision but at least it's an honest one. I know what you're going through. I've been there as a player. But how you all react is crucial to how far we go in this tournament because it's a part of making the whole camp focused and prepared. Plus, you've got to be up for it when you're called upon.'

I really did know what they were going through. I was left on the bench during the 1982 World Cup despite, I believed, being on top of my form. It was a blow. But in my opinion every player faces a choice under those circumstances: do you selfishly think of yourself, or do you accept it and help build the team spirit? I don't think I've ever sat on the bench moping and aggrieved at international level because it all comes down to the coach's decision – what he's looking for and what he feels is right for the team. At that time we played a flat back four, four across midfield and two up front. I always felt that put us in chains. Being the type of player I was it was very difficult for me to play at my best in that system. My international career would probably have been very different had I played in the era of another manager. Now I'm the coach making the sort of decisions that Ron Greenwood and Bobby Robson made about me. As a coach you do begin to appreciate why certain players – me included – didn't play and why certain players did.

Anyway, the message seemed to get through. There was some lively banter among the players on that Tuesday. The spirit that had characterized our World Cup campaign before the Romania game had returned. We trained well, doing some work on the shape of the team to face Colombia (although we didn't take too much out of the players who had played the previous day). It reinforced my belief that I had a good bunch of lads who would learn from the setback. If we got through to the last sixteen everyone would be on a high again.

During the day the security staff had spotted and ejected a foreign-based photographer in the bushes behind the hotel. He was escorted away by the gendarmerie and two policemen on horses. Later in the day we discovered they hadn't confiscated his pictures, which turned up in London, to the anger of the English photographers in La Baule, who never invaded our privacy.

One of the pictures showed Paul Scholes playing head tennis with one of his hands bandaged. He'd got it stamped on during the game in Toulouse. Inevitably we got several calls at the hotel during the day from Manchester suggesting he was either on the way home, or had even arrived at home. It's amazing how these rumours start.

Scholesy was certainly in my plans for the Colombia game, although I wanted to wait until we had tested Paul Ince's ankle before picking the side. We had to be convinced that Incey's ankle was fine; we had planned to test him on the Thursday morning, and run through the set-plays once we knew what the starting eleven was. Immediately after that we would travel to Lens's stadium, Stade Félix Bollaert, for a gentle forty-five-minute training session, as there was just a four-day gap between the two games. I made sure the players knew the schedule so that their minds were focused on match day again. Mine certainly was, despite the defeat. I hadn't read a paper, I had no idea what the press were saying, nor did I care. The only thing I cared about was that we were ready for Colombia.

I was under no illusions. I knew it was going to be a difficult game, but I was sure we were going to get through. Mind you, nothing I'd have said would have impressed the media. I wasn't popular as far as they were concerned for keeping Michael Owen out of press conferences before the match. He had talked to everyone after making such an impact against Romania, and although the media inevitably claimed that I was being obstructive in refusing them access, the reality was that Michael felt he'd done his fair share and didn't want to do anymore.

It was frustrating, but nothing could dent my positive mood, which had been helped by a phone conversation with Eileen Drewery the previous night. She was extremely positive. I was hoping that she might see Incey if his ankle didn't respond, and I was intending to ask all the players if any of them wanted to see her. I found myself wishing she was out in France with us (prior engagements back home had prevented her from coming out so far) since I was sure that she could play her part in the World Cup, be it with physical or mental support.

Scotland's fans could probably have done with some mental support that night. The fate of Craig Brown's side was sealed by a 3–0 defeat against Morocco. We had sent another message of good luck to Craig Brown in the dressing room in St Etienne – a dressing room that I hoped we would soon be using: the Geoffroy Guichard Stadium was to be the venue for the second-round match between the winners of Group H and the runners-up of Group G.

The next day – for the first time in a fortnight – I snatched an hour to listen to my Sony Walkman; a bit of Celine Dion, a bit of prayer, a big switch-off for my mind. After dinner I took a silly bet on the Paraguayan keeper Chilavert to score against the Spanish. He never came over the halfway line! I should have backed Paraguay to win because they knocked out Spain and the bookies made another killing. It was bad news at the end of a good day.

I woke up on the Thursday, the day before the game against Colombia, feeling no nerves and totally confident. My first thoughts were to find out if Paul Ince and Sol Campbell were fit. John and I watched Alan Smith put them through a very stringent test. Incey's ankle problem was the big concern, while Sol had tweaked his knee. We had to be sure: we couldn't go into the game with anyone less than 100 per cent fit, and I had to intervene on a couple of occasions to satisfy myself about Paul. But they both came through OK. It was a good start to the day.

The players, I knew, were looking forward to the game. We had shown them a video of Colombia and highlighted how much space they tended to leave on their flanks; how, if we pressurized them, they would give the ball away. We showed it to them time and time again. If ever a video worked in our favour, that was it, because the boys seemed very positive afterwards. I think they picked up on my mood. I remember Bobby Robson and Ron Greenwood's anxiety unnerving the squad when I was a player. But I didn't feel any anxiety at all.

Neither did John. He and I are very similar in the way that we approach games. We're very positive. Sometimes, if there's a gut feeling like there was against Romania, we try not to discuss it. Our relationship is quite instinctive. We complement each other. As soon as we went to Swindon together it was evident that we had different personalities, but that we got on very well. To say that we take no energy from one another would be one way of explaining how close we are; in other words, we're on the same wavelength. He's enthusiastic on the training ground – second to none – and the players respond to that. It certainly helped when I took over as England coach, when the players were obviously thinking: 'Well, what's this manager going to be like? What are his coaching staff like? What type of training are we going to do? What's his approach? Is he this, is he that?'

It was said in some quarters, when we first took over, that John didn't have the expertise or the experience that some of the other coaches had. But that's just not true – he has a great perception. John's got a very different type of gift: he's a wonderful communicator who brings the best out of the players. Just ask them, his coaching is always enjoyable. That's why the balance is so right. You must have a coach who the players can respond to, and John gets a response from the players in a unique way. To those who claim that I'm at a disadvantage because I've surrounded myself by people who haven't had experience at the highest level of football, I'd say that the two don't always go hand in hand. Look at Bobby Charlton and Bobby Moore. They were both World Cup winners yet neither of them made good managers.

They just weren't cut out for it. Besides, Ray, Peter Taylor and I have all played at international level. You don't play as many internationals as we did and not gain experience from it. Plus Dave Sexton was scouting for us and involved with the Under-21s, and he has bags of experience, too.

The bottom line is that the balance has to be right. Ours was. The spirit in our camp was marvellous and whenever I saw anyone's mood dipping a bit I just asked John, Clem, Glenn Roeder or Peter Taylor to give them a lift. As a leader of people trying to achieve something big you have to be aware of every situation and have your finger on every pulse.

As soon as we knew Incey and Sol were going to make the team we had a second session of set-plays and I told the players the line-up. David Batty would be dropping out and Becks would get his chance from the start in midfield. But I knew the main story back home would be that Michael Owen was going to play from the start in place of Teddy Sheringham.

David Batty was disappointed but he took it OK. He knew the situation. I think all the players were aware that sometimes I had to change the team for tactical reasons, not because somebody had had a poor game. Teddy understood too. They had seen the videos, seen how flat and square Colombia played at the back, how the game cried out for somebody in midfield who could see the right ball quickly. There was no-one better in our squad than David Beckham at doing that. David Batty does a fantastic job defensively, and his passing is wonderfully efficient. David Beckham's forward passing is better than David Batty's, but he hasn't got Batty's experience at winning the ball back, although he's getting better at it. He had come on against Romania and played the right game for us. Yet I had always earmarked him for the Colombia game. I had been waiting a long time to be able to play Darren Anderton and David Beckham in the same team – eighteen months in fact. I knew what they could give us:

both could play wide and both could play inside. If I'd had that time to work on the pairing we would hopefully have reached a stage where you wouldn't know who was playing wide and who was playing inside.

As for Michael – I had earmarked him for this game, too. He was always going to play, even if Teddy had scored two goals and played a blinder against Romania. We knew how many problems Michael could cause the Colombians at the back with his pace.

With the team chosen, we were up and running. The mood was good. Everybody seemed to want to get on with the job. Later, the staff had a vigorous game of head tennis and there was lots of good banter. Ray Clemence was hilarious.

We had got into a routine for our excursions from La Baule to our games: a light workout in the morning; lunch; packing; coach to St Nazaire. As we left on that Thursday, Yannick (the hotel manager) waved us off with both arms in the air and a double thumbs-up. The next day was a cup tie, no more no less.

On the short forty-five-minute flight to Lille (we would complete the journey to Lens by coach) both John and I managed a bit of shut-eye. It wasn't necessarily sleep. I also used some time during the flight to pray. The players seemed outwardly very relaxed, but I could tell they were focused, too, that they had got over the disappointment of Romania. The card schools were busy, with Alan Shearer, David Batty, Rob Lee and Tim Flowers heavily involved as usual. The Manchester United boys – Gary Neville, Becks and Paul Scholes – were sitting more quietly at the front of the plane. Tony Adams and Merse spent the time reading.

It was a lovely sunny Thursday evening when we arrived in Lens on the coach, having replaced the 'Oman Football Association' pennant in the front window with one of our own! On the motorway, we passed the Colombians going in the other direction. The Stade Félix Bollaert had a very

English feel about it. Surrounded by streets of terraced houses, it reminded me of Goodison Park, although there were rather more trees around.

I had intended to break off before the end of training to do my press conference, but once I got involved, that idea went by the board. I enjoyed joining in with the players in the evening sunshine and getting a feel for the stadium. When I did finally get to talk to the press, the first question – from a Canadian TV journalist – was a corker. 'Coach,' he said from the back of a crowded room, 'If Michael Owen was the Beatles, and Teddy Sheringham was the Rolling Stones, whose tune would you be whistling in the shower in the morning?' I'd thought of my answer halfway through the question. 'I've always liked the Beach Boys,' I replied, which set the tone for an easier session than I'd expected.

I felt relaxed, and I knew the English press were probably thinking that I looked too relaxed for a coach on the eve of a make-or-break game. I also knew – and it didn't surprise me – that an approach had been made to the chairman of The F.A. by a couple of journalists wanting to know whether my job was on the line if, say, we were to lose 1–0 against Colombia. Well, the fact was that The F.A. wanted me to stay on as England coach for Euro 2000 at least, so if they were trying to build up the pressure on me, they didn't succeed. Anyway, I felt too confident that we were going to win for them to knock me off my perch.

It was a fifty-minute drive to the Chateau Tilques outside Lens where we were staying. I shared a car with David Davies, and both of us laughed as we surged past signs that proclaimed 'Calais 68km' then 'Calais 34km' and so on. We imagined the headlines that might follow if we kept going and turned up there – 'Hoddle Heads Home Shocker', and the rest. I wasn't ready for that.

However, life didn't prove quite as peaceful at the Chateau Tilques as we might have hoped. It was certainly beautiful, but also very rural as we found to our cost the following morning. Some of us were woken by ducks and a donkey, while others were serenaded by a cockerel. Brian Scott was rushing round near the part of the hotel where the players were staying trying to find the noisy bird at 5 a.m. The things you do for your country!

Our policy of keeping the tabloid papers out of reach of the players backfired somewhat on our first morning at the chateau. The boys came down for breakfast to find that the staff had decided to try to please us by buying in vast quantities of English papers. Thankfully, they were quickly withdrawn to a back room. Only after the match did I find out that they contained some vicious attacks on me, despite the fact that it was the eve of such an important match. One read: 'Of all the sides in France, England are the most unhelpful. I have known Glenn Hoddle for many years. There is no question he has changed. He has become insular and will not let anyone inside his thinking. For an England coach, a public property, that is disastrous. I have supported him down the line. But though, not once, has he said thank you, that support will run out if he gets it wrong and England go out. For England not to qualify provides only one conclusion. That his job is too big for him. He'd have to go.'

Reading that, perhaps people will understand why the tabloid press can be so damaging to one's preparations for vital matches. That's why it's important not to read them. (But I wouldn't be human if I wasn't angry to discover that the article had been written by a journalist who has made money by writing an unauthorized book about me that I wasn't happy about, and who had to be forced to stop referring to himself as a family friend.) He's the one that has changed, not me. He's the one who was asking the chairman whether my job was on the line the day before the Colombia game. But that's journalism and some journalists for you.

There was something more pleasurable to read over

lunch, namely a fax from Prince Charles wishing us good luck and letting us know that he and Prince Harry were coming to the game. I got the Doc, with his very proper English accent, to read it out to the players. They were chuffed.

The journey to the game later that Friday afternoon took almost an hour. We were accompanied by the usual fleet of motorbikes in front of us, a helicopter overhead and the security guards on board. John and I still managed to shut our eyes for a while, despite the loud music pounding out from the coach's cassette player (including a recording of Queen's 'We are the Champions'). I must have needed the sleep because I nodded off for about twenty minutes. But I felt really good when I woke up. And as we came into the stadium the atmosphere was wonderful and our support was huge. This time I felt that it was going to be our night.

The dressing room was relaxed, too, although we couldn't help but notice that young Michael Owen was quieter than he had been before the games in which he'd been starting on the bench. You could hardly blame him; this was his big moment. We had the music going as usual. Les Ferdinand's tapes were a big hit. Les certainly knows where it's at musically; Incey and I were watching him dancing as he was getting changed. He couldn't help it. It was great to watch.

After the warm-up everyone was geeing each other up and there were the usual last-minute things to go over with the players. I wanted to remind them about the referee as late as possible. We were a little bit worried about the Mexican ref – he'd sent three off earlier in the tournament. So just before we went down the tunnel I shouted out to everyone, 'Don't get booked for something stupid.' And I made a point of saying to Sol Campbell, who was already on one yellow card, 'If you're going to get booked, make sure it's for something the team needs rather than anything silly, because that will put you out of the next game.' I didn't want him booked for back-chat to the referee or for something trivial like throwing the ball away. If he got booked because he mistimed a tackle, that was a different story. You can't go out there with the attitude: 'Oh, I can't touch anyone.' You've got to play your natural game. But I wanted him to realize that he couldn't take any chances.

There were many high spots in the game, but the overall performance pleased me the most, even if we did lose our way a little bit in the second half when Incey began to drop too deep and we lost the urgency of our first-half performance. David's free-kick was a cracker. It was quite far out but somehow I knew he was going to score. Sometimes you get a feeling about these things. As for Darren Anderton, he was superb. He'd taken such unjust criticism and stick from the media and fans, so I was thrilled for him. I stuck by him and rightly so; he's a good player who's blessed with natural ability. He gives us balance. He plays the game with his head up, and he plays it intelligently. He's also a naturally fit athlete, which helped him recover quickly from what was a very long lay-off. He was worth the risk. He knew and I knew that if he broke down there was nothing we could do about it. But the World Cup only comes round every four years and I always felt that I could nurture his undoubted talent and bring it out of him pretty quickly. So when he scored that first goal I felt like sticking a few fingers up at certain people myself. It was the perfect way to answer the critics.

David Batty and Steve McManaman did well, too. We already knew what David could do, but Steve came on at a time when I felt that we needed some fresh legs to get forward and he did everything that we asked of him. I knew he'd run with the ball and he had the perfect platform to do so since we were 2–0 up at that stage. I expect Pelé was wondering why I hadn't used Steve more often – he's one of his biggest fans.

We had earmarked where we thought we could nullify

the Colombian threat and win the ball, and our plan worked to perfection on the night. We knew that they were skilful and would make life hard for us, but the players really fancied having a go at the Colombians because they knew that if they won the ball, the counter-attack was on. With Michael's pace, that was always going to make for an exciting game. We also knew the wing-backs were going to get loads of space because their key midfielders, Rincon and Valderrama, just didn't want to play wide. Consequently, once we'd won the ball our wing-backs could break into the space early. Darren had so much space that in the end Scholesy could just shut his eyes and clip the ball out to the right-hand side because he knew Darren would be there.

Colombia were such an eye-of-the-needle side: they would rarely get round the outside to get crosses in, preferring to build up from the back without any width in midfield at all. We had detailed Incey, Becks and Scholesy to win the ball back and press them higher up the pitch. Because they didn't play with three at the back they had fewer options when they brought the ball out of defence. They were very flat.

In the end most of the play went down their right because Valderrama didn't play wide. However, that just added to what seemed to be the general perception that England were much stronger on the right than the left. One of the criticisms of my squad selection was that I only took one naturally left-footed player – Graeme Le Saux – to France. But I didn't have much choice since the only other naturally left-footed player in serious contention, Andy Hinchcliffe, was injured. Phil Neville was off form and is naturally right-footed anyway. But we'd known for a while that there is a shortage of left-sided players in the country at the moment, both on the wing and at full-back. Fortunately there are some promising young players coming through at Under-21 level.

Of course we had contingency plans in case Graeme got

injured. Robert Lee had played that position for us; Darren Anderton could play there, too (if that had happened then Becks would have played on the right). We could also have played 4-4-2 with McManaman in midfield protected by a full-back, and we'd had a look at young Rio Ferdinand in that position. So we were prepared for anything. But there was no reason not to persevere with Graeme Le Saux. He'd played well against Tunisia, and although he made two mistakes against Romania that cost us, for most of the game he had had the upper hand on Dan Petrescu. It was his concentration that had been lacking. There was nothing wrong with his performance against Colombia either.

It was a great feeling when the whistle went, although I was disappointed we hadn't scored more goals. Considering the way we played, and some of our movement just after half-time, we could have had four or five. We could have torn them apart. Michael, in particular, will feel he should have scored when he was through on goal, but the chance fell on his weaker left side. I remember thinking, as he went down the inside-left channel and shaped to shoot, 'That's his weak ankle.' Consequently, he didn't take the chance. We had found out about the weakness by default. I had wanted to work on his left side in the build-up to the World Cup but we discovered that he'd had an ankle problem on his left side for eighteen months and he needed to do strengthening work on it at first. Thank goodness we found out – we could have made it ten times worse. He worked in the gym every day to strengthen the ankle before we started working him intensely on his left side and there was a big improvement. But there's still a slight fear in his mind; injuries can affect a player like that. The good thing is that we've addressed the problem and have hopefully brought him on. Twenty minutes of finishing on his left side four days a week should do the trick.

Although it was a bit frustrating to score just two goals

after dominating the game, on reflection I decided it was no bad thing to hold something back for Argentina, who now lay in wait. I had been vaguely aware during the game that the Tunisians were leading 1–0 against Romania – if it had stayed that way we would have won the group and played Croatia – but the score in that game didn't mean anything to me. I was too focused on our match. Besides, although I would have liked to have won the group, that was only for our own satisfaction. The identity of our next opponents didn't bother me at all. I knew that each side would offer a different set of obstacles. Croatia had skilful players and were a wonderful counter-attacking side who were getting stronger all the time. We knew all about Argentina. It would be a tough game whoever we played. So when we were given the signal that the Romanians had got an equalizer it didn't change our attitude at all.

Of course, those flash interviews are a lot easier when you've won, despite the fact that I had lost my voice shouting instructions to the players. They were buoyant in the dressing room afterwards, really high. Everyone was congratulating each other. I was very proud to be English that night. The support was absolutely magnificent, every bit as good as it had been four days earlier in Toulouse.

We finally pulled into the long driveway of the chateau around 2 a.m. There were so many English cars on the road back to Calais that we could have been back on the M25. They were beeping their horns and waving flags from their windows. It was tremendous. The coach bringing our families and friends had joined the convoy en route, and was behind us. We had decided that this would be the right time for them to stay overnight: if we were out of the tournament we would all need the support, and if we had qualified then we could all enjoy each other's company.

When all the travelling was done, we could celebrate. There were drinks – champagne included – then dinner for everyone. Many of the staff sat up until after 3 a.m. Vanessa was there, although she hadn't been to the game, and David Davies' wife Susan had us all in hysterics with her jokes. It was a lovely break in a campaign that we hoped still had more than two weeks to run.

CHAPTER 11

THE CALM BEFORE THE ARGENTINIAN STORM

27 – 29 JUNE 1998

Although we had beaten Colombia and won through to the last sixteen of the World Cup, we still had to train. If the players thought they were going to be able to sleep off the celebrations of the previous night, they were wrong. After all, we had the match of our lives in four days' time. I have to admit I expected a bit of a reaction after the festivities of the previous night but the players were as professional as they had been throughout our campaign. There were no grumbles at all.

It was another 'private' session at a secret venue fifteen minutes from the chateau. John took the players who had been involved against Colombia and gave them a good stretch, before dividing them into teams for some head tennis. It was nice and relaxed – a good session. Peter Taylor, Glenn Roeder and I took the players who hadn't played. I always tried to do that the day after a game. It gave me a chance to see who, if anyone, was down in the dumps. As it turned out, a couple of them did need lifting, but they were really up again after that session. I told them, again, as I'd told them before, that they were just as important as the starting eleven, particularly given the amount of goals that had been scored in the World Cup during the last twenty minutes of games. Any sub had to be more than just physically ready to come on. They had to know the shape, the tactics and the set-plays. Sometimes subs don't realize just how big a part they have to play.

After the session we had lunch with the wives and girlfriends, who weren't due to leave until later that afternoon. It was a lovely day in a great setting – apart from the English weather. It absolutely belted down with rain, so much so that only Nigel Martyn and the Doc took the scheduled shopping trip to St Omer. Nigel was on the lookout for baby clothes for his new daughter who was born during the week. He had flown back for the birth and then rejoined us before the Colombia game.

There were plenty of pictures of the girls in the press on that Saturday morning, taken as they left Waterloo on Eurostar the day before. Fortunately, the accompanying headlines weren't quite as bad as we'd expected, despite the inevitable references to 'Lovetrains', etc.

We were forced to shelter from the rain under the open boot of our coach as we waved the wives and girlfriends off that afternoon. I'm sure they must have wondered why we were in such good spirits as they left, but it was because Peter Taylor had got us going with 'Always Look on the Bright Side of Life'. I was sad to see Vanessa go. Half an hour later we were on the road ourselves, back 'home', as La Baule had become. At St Nazaire airport there were yet more camera crews to welcome us; yet more locals to wave to along the nearby roads; and a warm welcome from the hotel in the shape of a huge banner emblazoned with the words 'Welcome Home Great'!

As soon as I could I phoned my mum and dad, who were obviously delighted. Mum was so proud. We had a bit of a laugh because my dad had vowed that if England ever won the World Cup outside our own country he would run down his street naked. So I told mum to tell him to take another part of his clothing off. Meanwhile, there were messages coming in from all over the place. Everyone was thrilled. My kids had come out for the game and had absolutely loved it. They'd painted their faces and had the time of their lives.

The minute I put the phone down to my mum and dad David Davies told me I had another call to take – from the Buckingham Palace switchboard. I thought it was Steve Penk from Capital Radio doing another wind-up. I took some convincing that it was actually the Prince of Wales' private secretary. He told me that Charles and Harry were delighted with the result, and he called me 'Sir', to which I replied, 'Not until we win it, surely!' I was ready for the giveaway question and I was going to use my own Prince Charles impersonation (I'm quite good at it) but halfway through the conversation I realized that it really was Buckingham Palace. I said that we appreciated the call and that I'd pass the message on to the players and staff. I also said that we hoped to see Charles and Harry again – at the World Cup Final.

On the morning of Sunday 28 June, all twenty-two players trained, including Gareth and Incey. Three games into the tournament it was an encouraging roll call. The players already knew the team for Argentina: it would be unchanged from the line-up that had beaten Colombia. However, at the press conference only Alan Shearer, Darren and Scholesy were on parade. We kept Becks and Michael Owen under wraps at their request. Some players were starting to complain that they'd done more than their fair share with the media. Graeme Le Saux also asked not to be included, which was understandable considering his wife is of Argentinian origin. The media in England had been besieging her and her parents and Graeme was unhappy about it. In the past he'd been at ease with the media but he was starting to see another side. Michael Owen cheered him up by challenging him to a game of pétanque.

By this time we were already well advanced in our planning for St Etienne and Argentina. I hadn't had a chance to see them myself – we always seemed to be travelling when they were playing – but the videos were ready for viewing and we had the scouts' reports as well. I had said publicly that we were happier playing Argentina than Croatia and I had really meant it. Everyone seemed to think that Argentina were the tougher team, but I knew that Croatia were a very talented side who had really progressed from the one that had done so well during Euro '96. I think it would have been more difficult to play against them, despite the fact that we would have been hot favourites to win. Argentina were undoubtedly a good side, and a hard-working one, but I really fancied us to beat them. I also felt strongly that the chances that hadn't gone in against Colombia might go in against Argentina. It all added to my feeling that Argentina were better opponents for us than Croatia.

In any case, I had to look at the game from my players' point of view. I wouldn't have been much of a coach if I'd come out and said, the day before the game, that I wished we were playing Croatia. What would that have done for their confidence? It didn't really bother me which of the two teams we were playing, but if I could gain some psychological upper hand for the benefit of the players, then I would do so.

Of course, there was another reason for wanting to play Argentina: the media liked to call it revenge, but I preferred to describe it as redressing the balance. It was twelve years since that infamous World Cup quarter-final in Mexico and Maradona's 'Hand of God' goal, a match that had affected me more than any other game in my entire life. I was fifteen yards away from the ball when Maradona 'scored'. I didn't get over losing for days afterwards. I didn't blame Maradona, though. It was the officials who let the goal stand who really angered me. Twelve years later, perhaps things could be evened up.

I was sure I wasn't alone in having such thoughts. I expect that most of the nation felt the same way, not to mention the players, who I knew would be up for the game. John had actually asked some of them where they were when the 1986 game was played. Michael Owen had perked up and said, 'I think I was in my cot, John.'

But I was under no illusions about how tough playing Argentina in the second round would be, and about how much hard work we would have to put in to achieve our objective of winning the World Cup, the Final of which was now exactly two weeks away. We had watched Brazil beat Chile 4–1 in style on the Saturday night, and knew that we would have to take them on at some stage if we were to become world champions. But before that we had to win our second-round game. My feelings about Argentina were good – I just felt we were capable of winning the game.

We really only had one full day to prepare the players and focus on the game, because by the Monday we were to be on the move again, to St Etienne. But it wasn't a problem. We'd had a great session up in Lens the day after the Colombia game on a training pitch that was as good as any surface we had played on in the tournament. We'd also recorded a load of videos featuring all Argentina's set-plays, plus at least forty minutes of free-flowing play, to show the boys before our final light session prior to departure from La Baule.

The good news was that everyone was fit. Incey had come through from his ankle problem with flying colours, Sol had passed a late fitness test and even Gareth was fine. I wasn't convinced he was 100 per cent fit but he came through a very good session with the boys and did all the things that we asked of him, including twisting and turning. Of course, having played three games in eleven days, everyone was carrying a few knocks and bruises. Even David Beckham had what we call a tight thigh – lactic acid build-up – which meant that we had to take precautionary measures in practising our set-plays. Peter Taylor, who wasn't a bad crosser of the ball in his time, stood in for Becks, chipping the ball in so that we could work on the signals and runs off the ball. I wanted to change some of the set-plays – it was our fourth game, after all – and I knew that the forty-five-minute session at the stadium in St Etienne would be an open one and not the place to be changing tactics.

St Etienne seemed notably sunnier and warmer as we got off our plane and I felt relieved that the game kicked off at 9 p.m. rather than at 4 p.m. Our hotel at the airport was cosy at best, but it served its purpose for the twenty-four hours we were there. Finding accommodation at such short notice had been a nightmare for our travel manager, Brian Scott. The only really decent hotel he'd found in the area was too far away in Lyons. I remembered from my days playing for Monaco that the standard of the hotels in St Etienne wasn't too hot.

Still, we settled in as quickly as we could before leaving for our training session at the Geoffroy Guichard Stadium. I didn't have happy memories of that particular venue. I got injured there in my Monaco days and had to have a knee operation. The cartilage got infected – there was a million-to-one chance of that happening – and it ended up forcing me out of the game for two years and threatening my career. It was another motive for redressing the balance the following night.

I was delighted at how relaxed the lads looked during training, despite the number of television camera crews which seemed to have appeared – we counted almost thirty at the press conference afterwards. It wasn't a short conference, mainly because our Spanish and French interpreters both insisted on translating every word, regardless of the nationality of the questioner. It was also unbelievably hot under the barrage of lights and my throat, which had been suffering since the group games, was agony. I gave a thumbs-up to the BBC's Ray Stubbs who was at the back of the room. I'd done some interviews with him the previous night and my voice had totally gone so he'd given me some Fishermen's Friends. I had about six or seven of them in my pocket and just kept reaching down for them. Ray couldn't work out why I kept putting my thumbs up and pointing to my throat, but in the end he realized. Those Fishermen's Friends really had come up trumps.

Despite the best efforts of the media, I still wouldn't use the word 'revenge' in relation to the game with Argentina. However, a question prompted by Alf Ramsey's instruction to the England players to refuse to swap shirts with the Argentinians in 1966 nearly led to me scoring a diplomatic own goal. I said that of course I would allow the players to swap shirts, but not until after the game. The English press laughed and the Spanish interpreter set about his task. I had no idea what he was saying, but was rescued by Giancarlo Gavarotti, an Italian journalist, who explained that I had been misinterpreted as refusing to let the players swap shirts at all. If it had been reported like that, we could have had a major problem even before the game had started. The press seemed excited that we were going to be playing in all-white, as England did in that famous 1966 victory over Argentina. The truth is that it came about only after discussions with FIFA, but I was pleased too.

During the press conference – and the breaks for interpretation – we could see a TV monitor showing the Germans keeping their World Cup campaign alive. Again they came back from being a goal down, this time to Mexico. It was the same lesson as always – you have to be at your very toughest and most determined once you've taken the lead against the Germans.

The Dutch joined them in the quarter-finals later that night. We all watched their game against Yugoslavia, a match in which Dennis Bergkamp clearly stamped on a Yugoslav player in the corner. When it happened, I immediately thought he would get a red card. But amazingly he got away with it. It was typical of the inconsistent refereeing at the World Cup, as Zinedine Zidane had been sent off for exactly the same thing when France played South Africa.

Later on that night I sat outside enjoying a couple of beers and a good chat with the staff. I felt good. We'd done all the preparation, the players were fit and the atmosphere was very relaxed, despite the enormity of the game the following day. Another good sign was that Ray Clemence was back on the beer. He'd been on water for the last two games but that night he had a couple of pints and went to bed a happy man. So did I, but it was nothing to do with alcohol. It was because there were now only two World Cup quarter-finals places left up for grabs, and I felt very, very confident that one of them would be ours.

CHAPTER 12

ARGENTINA–DEJA VU

30 JUNE 1998

England's players had never been as well prepared for any game as they were for the match against Argentina. I say that with real confidence. By Tuesday 30 June, a day that dawned hot and dry, they had no need to train any more. They had done enough. Instead, we put them through some gentle stretching exercises in the grounds of the hotel, well out of sight of any stray photographers. The boys had a huge game ahead of them and didn't need people peering through camera lenses at them while they tried to clear their minds.

At least twelve players took up the option of vitamin injections to boost the supplements that all the players had taken. Most of the players recognized how valuable the supplements had been as they were now feeling the benefit of Dr Rougier's advice. Some of them had mentioned how full of energy they felt, even in the last five minutes of a game. The sprints I noticed Alan Shearer making in the last few minutes of the Colombia game backed that up. Alan looked as fresh as if the match had only just kicked off.

As the kick-off was not until 9 p.m. local time, we had several hours during the afternoon in which to try to relax, to switch off physically – you can never switch off mentally – from the massive game that lay ahead of us. The players rested, while some of the coaches opted for a spot of sunbathing around the swimming pool. Peter Taylor and I had a quick game of table tennis. I can play a bit when I put my mind to it.

It may sound like a contradiction in terms, but that period before a game is actually the most relaxing part of the preparation. It's the lull before the storm, so to speak. We'd done everything we could. We'd had all the meetings, watched all the videos, done all the training. We were confident; we were getting stronger as the tournament wore on.

Meanwhile the Romanians went out of France '98 after losing 1–0 to Croatia in a game that perfectly illustrated the ups and downs of football. Watching Dan Petrescu getting substituted late on in that game, I felt for him. One minute the player I signed for Chelsea was a hero after scoring that late winner against us; the next minute he – and his country – were out of the World Cup. I had made a point of seeing Dan to congratulate him after our game against Romania. We had a bit of banter about his goal. I pretended to punch him, but really we had a hug and wished each other good luck for the rest of the tournament. Of course I wasn't pleased that he'd scored against us – I was gutted. But the moment I saw him score I just knew I had to see him afterwards. And now the Romanians, with their bleached blond hair, were out of the World Cup.

We were ten minutes late leaving for the stadium because Dr Rougier was giving Incey his vitamin injection. It didn't matter. In the end we arrived bang on time. I said to John, 'You watch, there'll be more Argentinians in the crowd than there will be English.' The Argentinians, of course, had been based in St Etienne and knew they'd be staying there if they won their group. John had looked at me as if he didn't quite believe me, but when we got inside the ground he saw I was right. It was full of Argentinians. They were doing this song and dance all around the stadium, and we had a bit of a joke about it. Glenn Roeder said to me, 'I don't know if they've been to see Dr Rougier, but if they can last ninety minutes jumping up and down like that ... ' I think my reply was something about peaking too early! But it was a pretty amazing scene. They'd all taken off their shirts and were swinging them around their heads, swaying from side to side – I'd never seen anything like it. It was really energetic. But by the time kick-off came the support was pretty evenly balanced. I think that there were just as many English fans in the stadium but that our colours weren't as striking as their sky blue.

I spent the hour before the game going round the players. The key was to try to strike a balance between, on the one hand making sure the players all knew their duties, and on the other, keeping it as relaxed a dressing room as possible. We spoke about the lack of height in the Argentinian team; we spoke about set-plays, about how important it was to get a good delivery into the box as we felt we could profit in that area. The music was playing as usual – I think it was the same tape belonging to Les Ferdinand that we had used before the Colombia match. As far as I could tell, not one of the players looked tense or out of sorts. They looked focused. They looked fit. And they looked determined to get a good result. It wasn't complacency. It was a strong vibe that this was a game we were going to win.

Of course, the start wasn't quite what we had hoped for. In fact, to concede a penalty after just six minutes was nothing short of a nightmare. My alarm bells started ringing as the ball was dropped in behind our defence, but there were so many bodies getting across that I couldn't actually see what was happening. I saw David Seaman's body go down, and the next minute I knew there was an appeal and with a sinking heart I saw the referee point to the spot. I asked Clem, who was sitting further up the bench, whether he'd seen it. He said he wasn't sure about it. But it was immaterial: the ref had said it was a penalty and all we could do was hope David saved it. Clem and I looked at John, who said, 'Well, he knows where it's going.' Time and time again we had shown the three keepers – Dave, Nigel and Tim – a video featuring some of Argentina's penalties, including the one Batistuta had scored against Jamaica. We had shown it to them once more on the morning of the match. We were sure that Batistuta was going to hit the penalty across his body to the keeper's right. I was just praying. I looked at David, willing him to remember. 'Now's the time Dave,' I was thinking. Of course, he did remember. Batistuta did hit it to Dave's right and Dave got a good hand on it, too. That's where your preparation comes in. He was so close to saving it.

I felt numb. We all just looked at each other and I stood up and went to the side of the pitch to try to get a message to the players. I said to Graeme Le Saux, who was the nearest, 'Tell the players to keep their shape. And don't panic. There's plenty of time left.'

It all unfolded after that. What a first half of football it was. Forty-five minutes of unbelievable drama. We were sitting on the bench trying to take everything in, feeling that we were doing OK. We bounced back pretty quickly after their goal. There was an urgency about our game. Suddenly, Michael Owen got himself into a position ... and we just screamed. We were all screaming on the bench. Take him on, get at him. And the boy did absolutely brilliantly to take the defender on. It showed his maturity. It was as if he was saying, 'I'm going past you because I've got the pace to go past you, and you've got two options. You let me go and I score, or you bring me down and you might get sent off.'

Watching what happened, I went through a range of

emotions. I saw Michael touch the ball past the player and go down, and the referee give the penalty. I have to admit I wasn't convinced at the time that it was a penalty. It could have been from where I was sitting, but in my heart I wasn't sure. It certainly wasn't cast-iron. But my immediate reaction was, 'Great, maybe that's a bit of justice.'

Michael did the right thing. There's no way I would ever tell a player to go down in the box, to dive in order to earn a penalty. What I would tell him is that if an opponent physically catches you then stay on your feet if you can; if not, if you've been fouled, go down. That's professionalism. Most other countries recognize this. I think we get far fewer free-kicks than others because of the efforts our players make to stay on their feet. If you're fouled you should get your just rewards. Of course, there are certain times when you tell a striker to go across a defender, who's then got the option of bringing the striker down or letting him go. That's not cheating, that's intelligent play. That's exactly what Michael did.

I was thrilled that we had the chance to get back on level terms so quickly, but I'd noticed something else. For their penalty David Seaman had been booked for bringing the Argentinian player down, so I was expecting the defender who'd brought Michael Owen down to get a yellow card at least, if not a red. But nothing happened. I was looking at the referee and at the fourth official, to whom I said, very politely, 'Where's the card? Red, yellow, where is it?' I couldn't understand how David could have been booked for being the last man and bringing their forward down, yet their last man had got off without punishment. It should have been a sending off according to the new interpretation. Again, it was down to the referee. But in my opinion he had been inconsistent.

There was very little I could do from the bench, but I did get Incey to have a word with the referee because I could see no-one else had realized the injustice of what had gone on.

Of course, when Incey went up to the referee to explain to him, what did the ref do? He booked Paul Ince. That's when I went absolutely berserk at the fourth official. I was so mad that I was sitting down when Alan was running up to take the penalty, and still sitting when the ball hit the back of the net and the boys were jumping up all around me. I was absolutely outraged at what had – or rather hadn't – happened. At that point I thought perhaps it was a sign that something was going to go very wrong.

Later on in the game the fourth official, a Norwegian, turned to me and said, 'Glenn, what can I do?' I just said, 'I understand you can't do anything, but you have to ask the referee at half-time why he didn't take action against their defender. You know what I'm saying is right. You must talk to him.'

After that incident I was really uneasy, even though I was naturally delighted we had pulled it back to 1–1. In my mind it was game on. And although it was always going to be a tight game I was pleased with the way we were playing. There was a good spring in our step. Darren was getting plenty of the ball, Becks was just starting to get a couple of passes going, and young Michael was buzzing from winning the penalty. The defence was doing its job, too, trying to squeeze out their dangerman, Ariel Ortega. We had decided beforehand that we weren't going to man-mark Ortega. We knew we couldn't, not with the new rules. You were asking for trouble if you thought you could man-mark for ninety minutes and stay on the pitch. Besides, we had shown the players a video in which Ortega continually lost the ball whenever he received it with bodies around him, so we detailed Incey to patrol alongside him in the midfield. But for our plan to work, the gap between Paul Ince and David Beckham, and our back three – in what I call the corridor – needed to be kept very narrow indeed.

However, Ortega – who's a very shrewd player – kept just

drifting out wide, away from the hub of the midfield, where Incey didn't really want to follow. So at times we had to defend three against three, which we could handle when we were on the attack and the ball was sixty yards away but was a problem whenever they were sneaking off the back of us and getting into that corridor. That's when I felt uneasy. When other players were on the ball, I didn't feel there was any danger. But when Ortega started running at us, it was a different story.

Having said all that, I didn't think Ortega was the world-class player everyone made him out to be. He's a dangerous little player but as a creator of chances, I think we've got better. What about Michael Owen, for starters? No-one was thinking about Ortega after Michael had scored his wonderful goal. The way he took it was inspired, but the fact that it stemmed from counter-attacking play (hitting the opposition on the break), something we'd been working on over the last eighteen months, was the marvellous thing. You need pace to carry it off, but we've got that in abundance. We'd spoken about winning the ball in the middle third as we did, from where Becks clipped a cute little early ball through the middle. Michael's first touch with the outside of his boot took him past the defender on the halfway line. After that he had just one thing on his mind. He went at their defence. His pace took him past a second defender and towards their sweeper, Ayala. It was at that point I sensed that something was on because Ayala plays so deep that if you get past him, you're in on goal. I knew Michael would go on his right side and when his acceleration took him past it was like lightning. He went past Ayala as if he was standing still. We've always been amazed at how fast he runs with the ball at his feet. A little dummy and he was just away on the outside of the last man. We were all off the bench screaming and willing him on.

Suddenly I was aware that Scholesy was steaming up on the outside. Now sometimes you can't see the angles from the

The opening minutes of our game against Argentina weren't quite what we had hoped for. We conceded a penalty (right), but then got our chance to equalize with a penalty of our own (below).

Michael Owen's fantastic goal was a stunning moment and one I'll never forget (above). This picture of David Seaman sums up how we all felt! (left).

(Colorsport, Allsport)

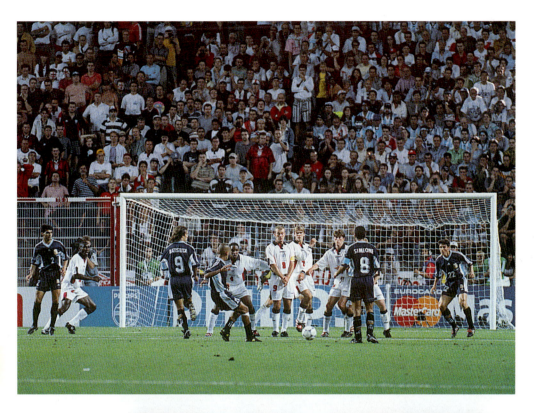

The free-kick
from which the
Argentinians
scored (above)
was a good one
and a set-play
we hadn't seen
before.
Throughout the
match, and the
tournament Sol
Campbell (left)
gave a
performance
that shows his
potential to
become one of
the top
defenders in the
world.

(ACTION IMAGES)

(Above) Beckham with Simeone, moments before the foul that led to his sending off (left). It all happened right in front of us, but much more importantly, in front of the referee.

(COLORSPORT, EMPICS)

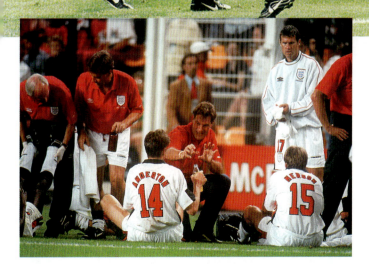

(Above) We thought we'd done it when Sol Campbell headed in his goal at the end of normal time. Unfortunately the referee, yet again, ruled against us. Minutes later I was talking to the players about extra-time and golden goals (above left). And so to penalties ... and David Seaman's save (left).

(COLORSPORT, EMPICS)

Incey and David Batty were up for taking penalties. As I watched David Batty run up to take the decisive kick I still thought we were going to win.
(Colorsport, Empics).

The final score (left). I was totally shocked but we had to get out on to the pitch and start picking people up (top). I can't even remember what I said to Gary Newbon (above) in the flash interview with ITV.

(Action Images, Empics, Mark Leech)

'I don't think we could have done any more.'

bench, and we were all thinking that Michael was going to give it to Scholesy who looked as if he had a straight-on view of goal. Then suddenly, as his body was falling away, Michael cut across the ball and hit it back across goal ... when it hit the net the feeling was fantastic. Unbelievable – for the boy, for us, for everyone. We were elated. It was a stunning moment and one I'll never forget. But, as a coach, I had to come down off that high very quickly, and ensure the players did the same. It had been such a wonderful goal that we could have easily conceded one immediately, through still having our heads in the clouds.

Once the game had settled down though, I sneaked a look at the Argentinian bench. They looked concerned. It made me feel good to think that psychologically we were on top because we were the first team to have scored against them in eight games, let alone go 2–1 up. It could have been even better minutes later when we might have buried them with the chance Scholesy missed.

That stemmed from a set-play. The Argentinians' lack of height meant Alan could win the first header from a straight goal-kick. They didn't have anyone who could handle him in the air. The plan was that Michael would make his move on the back of Alan getting the flick on, and that Scholesy would fill the hole Michael had left. It worked to perfection. It was our chance to kill them off. But I couldn't blame Scholesy. It was a more difficult chance than it looked. It was on his left side and the ball was running across him. His effort went just inches wide of the post. Until I saw it later on TV I didn't realize how close he was to the goal when he shot. He was about seven yards out. We thought it was more like twelve yards, but that's the view you get from the bench. We could have nailed them then. I doubt they'd have come back from 3–1 down.

Of course, fortunes can change so fast in football. One minute it was almost 3–1 in our favour, the next the

Argentinians had scored from a free-kick to level the scores at 2–2. From our point of view it was a terrible time to concede a goal, right on half-time. But what made it even more frustrating was that we could see it happening, almost in slow motion, from the bench, yet could do nothing about it.

It wasn't through want of trying. As they were shaping up to take it and our players were forming a wall, Peter Taylor was the first to react. 'Look down the wall,' he shouted. 'There's a danger man out wide.' At that moment we all looked and saw Ortega lurking off to the right alongside the wall. There was a big gap between him and Graeme, who was about fifteen yards from the end of the wall. We were all screaming. I was standing up and screaming, trying to alert Graeme to the danger. In a sense he was doing the right thing: he was aware of Ortega and knew he had to keep an eye on him, but the gap between them was too big.

It was a horrible feeling. John admitted afterwards that he had this sick, sinking feeling before they scored. He knew that they were going to score. You get an instinct like that sometimes. Of course, they took the free-kick and it hit the back of the net ... to be fair to them it was an excellent free-kick. But that didn't make it any easier to accept. My stomach just turned over.

The half-time whistle went almost immediately. Passarella, the Argentinian coach, must have had a great feeling going off while all I could do was be as positive as possible in the dressing room. Psychologically, I had to lift everybody. I thought that we had been the better side, that we had always looked threatening, and I told the players so. 'Cast your minds back to ten minutes into the game,' I said. 'We were 1–0 down. We are in a better position now than then. They've not let a goal in for eight games and you've put two goals past them in sixteen minutes. If we keep on playing like we have been then we'll win the game. Don't feel sorry for yourselves. There's nothing to be down about.'

I talked to them about the shape of the team, and warned them about not dropping off and letting Ortega run at us; whenever he had done that Argentina had looked dangerous. I also reminded them about our own set-plays. There had been one occasion in the first half when Tony Adams should have made a late run behind the wall, but the ball had been played elsewhere. We had planned it and worked on it often enough and it was annoying that it didn't happen. After that I just went round and talked to individual players. I said to Michael Owen, 'What a fantastic goal, son. Just go out there and try to reproduce your first-half performance.'

All the players were as positive going back down that tunnel as they had been at the start of the game. All except, perhaps, Graeme Le Saux. I think he was a little bit down. Ironically, he gave us an early call about some cramp in both his calves early in the second half. I suspect it might have been tension. I had spoken to him about his positioning at the free-kick. The most important thing was for him to defend our goal by tucking in and getting closer to the wall. Anything could have happened with Ortega positioned wide where he was: a cross, a run at goal … as it was they scored with, what was, I'm the first to admit, a wonderfully imaginative free-kick.

Just before the second half kicked off I went to the toilet and got a bottle of water. As I walked back down the tunnel I checked with John that we'd covered everything. I settled down to try to focus on the second half … but within seconds came the bizarre incident that was to transform the game. It involved Diego Simeone, the Argentinian captain, and, of course, our own David Beckham.

It happened right in front of us, but much more importantly, right in front of the referee. David got a whack from Simeone and went down. As he was lying on the ground I suddenly saw this foot – his foot – come out from nowhere. David's head was still down on the floor, and he hadn't even looked to see where Simeone was. He didn't even know he was there. If Simeone had walked just two yards away from David rather than stayed parallel with him, David's leg would have come out and kicked air. Of course Simeone made a meal of it, making it into something far worse than it was. But that doesn't excuse David. He should never have done what he did. When I saw it happen I just thought, 'What are you doing?' I thought about how many times we had warned him against that kind of behaviour, about reacting when provoked. It had been an issue ever since Le Tournoi, when a totally unnecessary booking had robbed him of the chance to play against Brazil.

However, I wasn't expecting a red card; I was expecting a yellow at worst. But it was red, for violent conduct. My stomach turned over again. How ever mad I was with David, I was furious with the referee. First, he hadn't produced a card for the tackle on Michael in the first half which gave us the penalty, and now this.

But I wasn't going to change the referee's mind. Nobody was. I had to get a grip. I had to concentrate on what I could change. I knew I would have to address the balance of the team. We had to cover ourselves. I had to decide whether to make a substitution immediately, or whether to wait and see how the game panned out. I thought about bringing David Batty on straight away to play alongside Incey in midfield. I even thought about taking one of the strikers off. However, I still wanted to try to win the game, be it during the ninety minutes or with a golden goal, and you can't win a game without strikers.

All sorts of things were running through my mind, and at that moment David Beckham wasn't one of them. Someone did go and see David in the dressing room but it couldn't be me. I knew I would have to deal with that problem after the game. All I remember is David untucking his shirt, looking back at the referee and walking off, his eyes staring straight ahead towards the tunnel. He didn't – or couldn't – look at me or anybody. It was a sad sight.

Now it was vital that we got the balance right because there was such a long way to go. So we decided to shift Darren into the midfield alongside Incey and pull Scholesy on to the left side of midfield. Gary Neville came over and I told him to tell Michael to play on the right side of midfield. Gary would give him protection from the full-back position. It meant that we would be playing with a back four, and four across the midfield defending in a line.

What I was planning to do when the game had settled down was rotate the two strikers, giving each of them five or six minutes at a time out on the right. It would have been unfair to Michael to stick him out there for the rest of the game because it is a position that calls for far more defensive responsibilities than a striker is used to. He would have had to track back constantly and we needed his pace up front. If you're going to get a goal with ten men you need to break with pace. But we also needed Alan's strength up front so I decided to compromise by rotating them. That way, the defender wouldn't get used to having one of them up front all the time. He might get used to Alan being up there but suddenly he's having to deal with Michael, who's totally different.

What surprised me was that the Argentinians didn't change their system. They kept their three at the back, they kept two very deep, they never tried to make an overlap, which was something we'd worked on at Bisham Abbey in case we had to play against ten men. I was pleased with that. I kept saying to John, 'Look, they're playing within us, they're playing inside our back four.' They never stretched us, which amazed me because if they had done we'd have been in trouble.

They kept attacking us through the middle and we kept making wonderful blocks, even though with twenty minutes to go we lost Graeme. He said that his calves had gone so we had to rejig and put Sol out at left-back. I was concerned about that. Graeme would have got forward and linked up with Scholesy better than Sol, but Sol shored us up at the back. Gareth went on too and put in a tremendous performance defending alongside Tony.

Tactically we couldn't have done much more than we did. The players couldn't have done much more either. How many times have you seen a game in which the team that gets a red card with seventy-five minutes to go hangs on for a result? It's very rare. The fatigue factor is usually too great – it's like playing for an extra thirty minutes.

To think that we very nearly won it outright in the ninety minutes ... I was convinced we had done. What a bizarre feeling it was when Sol's header went in, only for it to be disallowed for an alleged foul on their keeper. I've never felt like that before. I saw the ball go into their penalty area and I saw a challenge, but I certainly didn't see a foul. Then suddenly it hit someone – I didn't know it was Sol – and I saw the ball nestle in the back of the net. The feeling was incredible. I thought that was it, that we'd won. Everyone on the bench was on their feet. The special music that always greeted a goal came on. We'd done it. Several of the players, including Sol and Incey were off the pitch celebrating. Then ... horror. Out of the corner of my eye I saw the referee talking to the linesman and heard Clem say, 'He's not given it.' My stomach turned again, for the third time in the match. I just couldn't believe it. I turned and looked at the referee again. I suppose I was hoping that I had been seeing things. The goal had been disallowed. It got worse.

Argentina had taken the free-kick and gone on the attack, yet we still had four players off the pitch celebrating what they thought was the winning goal. John, Clem, Peter Taylor and I were screaming at them, trying to push them back on to the pitch as fast as possible. It was like the worst nightmare. I couldn't believe it was happening. It was as if someone had stopped the match and freeze-framed it. I thought, 'I know they are going to score. They are going to score.' And I remember they broke and it was two against one. Only Gary Neville was back for us. Luckily their player just overran it. If he had got in behind Gary who knows what would have happened. But Gary made a tremendous tackle. He gave it everything, and the ball spun off for a throw. It gave us time to regroup and get our balance back. For a minute I was wondering how long we had to hang on to our lead, the next thing I knew we were trying to hang on to the draw. My emotions went from being so high to being so low. It was the same for the players. But they had to drag themselves back into the game. The players had to concentrate. We had lost a goal just before half-time through lack of concentration. We couldn't let it happen again.

We didn't. We hung on to take the game into the thirty-minute extra-time period during which the first goal scored – the golden goal – would win the match. And we might have done just that had yet another decision not gone against us. We saw it straight away from the bench. We were up off our seats and out on to the pitch, we were so angry. What happened was that Alan Shearer went up for the ball with their defender, Chamot, and this guy's arm went above his head, above Alan's head, and handled the ball. I was in line with the referee, and the referee saw what we saw from the bench – that the handball was above Shearer's head. No-one could deny it. To make matters worse the defender went down and pretended he was injured. He knew that had the referee given a penalty, it might have decided the game. But it didn't matter because the referee appeared to decide that he had not seen the incident, which I found staggering. Compare it to some of the other penalty incidents in the World Cup. Italy, for instance, got lucky against Chile when Roberto Baggio just flicked the ball up and it hit a Chilean defender standing a yard away on the arm. I thought that was a terrible, terrible decision. There was no intent at all but that decision saved Italy on the day.

Although there had been an occasion in the first half when the referee could conceivably have given a penalty against Tony Adams after the ball hit him on the arm on the edge of the area the circumstances were vastly different. Then the ball had been flashed low across the box and there were loads of people in front of the referee. He could easily have missed the incident. Any offence there had to be accidental anyway. This time the ball had been travelling thirty or forty yards in the air towards Alan and the defender, whose arm was clearly in the air. (You have to ask yourself, 'What was his arm doing up there in the first place?')

I had had an uneasy feeling about the referee when he didn't book the defender for the challenge on Michael in the first half that led to our early penalty. Now, as then, I had a right go at the fourth official. I just could not believe the injustice of the decisions we were getting. But what can you do? You have to settle down on the bench and believe that things are still going to go your way. I did that, I genuinely felt that we would win the game right to the end. The referee's decisions kept knocking us sideways, but it didn't change my mind.

All the time we were trying to seek a balance between trying to hold on to the game, and trying to win it. We had to get the right people out there at the right time. I had to make a decision. I was worried that at some stage they would try and take us on the outside or start giving us problems from setplays. I had already replaced Scholesy with Paul Merson with twelve minutes of normal time remaining. It had been a toss-up between Merse and Steve McManaman. Macca would have given us some pace to break, but in the back of my mind I was thinking that if it went to penalties, Merse was Middlesbrough's penalty taker, whereas Macca didn't take them for Liverpool. At least we would have three men on the pitch who could take them. Darren Anderton, of course, would have made it four, but by the time we reached the shoot-out Darren had given way to David Batty. Darren had run and run and run. He'd worked his socks off, and I just felt it was time to shore things up. We needed the extra defensive legs, even though the back four were playing out of their skins. David would tighten things up alongside Incey and shield the back four, who could only defend like that for so long. There was no way, after everything that had happened, that I was going to lose the game through a golden goal. So halfway through the first period of extra-time I decided to send David on and see if we could take them to penalties.

There were three certainties for the penalties: Shearer, Owen and Merson, who all took them for their clubs. Of course, we'd have been confident of David Beckham sticking one in the back of the net ... but that option was no longer open to us. Teddy Sheringham has taken plenty of penalties, and he was one that I might have put on the pitch with five minutes to go. But we didn't dare take the risk. I had left two strikers on the pitch; to put another on would have been suicidal.

I could tell immediately from the reaction of some of the players that they weren't up for it. The defenders looked particularly unhappy. Tony and Sol were together. Sol was very fatigued. He was having a rub, a massage on his calves, and looked as if he'd had it. I asked Gary Neville if he was happy to go at number six. He said he was. Then there was Gareth. I said to him, 'You know it might come to it. You know you might have to take one.' He told me he'd be up for it, and I said, 'I'm sure you'll give it your best. You'll lay the ghost. It won't get that far, but if it does you'll have to be up there.' David Batty was up for it. He was very, very confident. He told me he'd never taken a penalty, but it didn't matter. I'd rather have someone who's up for it than someone who's not any day. Incey was up for it too. He'd had a fantastic game. He'd had to battle through and had put in a magnificent performance. They all had. Every single one of them.

In the end it came down to a list of five: Shearer, Ince, Merson, Owen and Batty. We had to submit the order of kickers to the referee beforehand. Once that was done there was no going back. But I never once thought that we weren't going to do it. Every fan must have felt the same way. We had played so well, had given our all. Surely now we deserved to get our just reward.

But the odds were stacked against us until the bitter end. The referee even ruled against us for the penalty shoot-out by ordering them to be taken at the end where the Argentinian fans were congregated. Initially it didn't bother me too much – kicking in front of your own fans can add extra pressure – but the trouble was that the Argentinian fans were throwing things at our players, and at Dave Seaman. I didn't see it, Peter Taylor did. I complained to the fourth official again but it was pretty futile – I really don't believe the referee was strong enough to do anything about it.

Alan, as I'd expected, scored our first penalty. It was a great penalty. He was never going to miss. Then, after David Seaman had saved their second effort, we had the chance to go 2–1 up. Incey had chosen to go at number two, which at the time I thought might suit us. It didn't. Incey's penalty wasn't good enough. What happened from then on is history. With hindsight I'd have put Michael or Merse at number two because if Incey had scored after Dave Seaman had made his save then their third kicker, Veron, would have been the one under pressure. But there was no way I could have predicted what was going to happen.

Merse and Michael, both seasoned penalty takers, put theirs away, and as I watched David Batty run up to take the decisive kick I still thought we were going to win. I saw it happen, I saw him miss. I couldn't believe it. Suddenly everything stopped. I was totally shocked. I had been so, so convinced that we were going to win, despite everything in the game having gone against us. I knew the pressure was on David. But I don't blame Incey and I don't blame David Batty. I don't blame any of the players. Paul Ince was magnificent on the night. He'd had a great World Cup. Someone was going to miss, whether it was one of them or one of us.

I had very little time to react, which was probably a good thing. I had to get out on to the pitch and start picking people up. All the coaching staff had to do the same. My immediate concern was the players, and in particular David Batty and Paul Ince. Incey was the most upset. David's a different type of character – not much fazes him. But considering what had just happened, the players were truly wonderful. They were clapping the fans. Everyone was very emotional. I looked up and saw my children, Zara and Jamie, in the stands. Anne was with them. I could see my uncle and my mate Dave Deller, too. That's when the enormity of what had happened hit me. I got all choked up and had to go down on my haunches out there in the middle of the pitch for about twenty seconds to pull myself together. The problem was that I hadn't been prepared to lose. It hadn't entered my mind.

After I had finished going round the players my next job was to go looking for Daniel Passarella. To be fair to him he was making his way over to me at the same time. He knew what a titanic battle it had been. We shook hands and embraced. The expression on his face said it all. He knew it had been a lucky way for them to go through and a cruel way for us to go out. But he was the one who was celebrating.

Within minutes of the game finishing I had to do a flash interview for ITV. Trying to get my head round it so soon after the game was nigh on impossible. It was the hardest interview I've ever done in my life. My emotions were all over the place. Apparently Gary Newbon asked me if David Beckham's sending off had cost us the game ... but I don't remember what I said in reply. All I know is that I answered the questions as well as I possibly could and tried to hold myself together. I knew I had to be strong. My stomach, which had turned over so many times during the game, felt as if it had been ripped out. And yet there I was standing by the pitch with all this noise going on around me and Gary Newbon screaming questions. At the same time I knew the nation was watching and listening back home and feeling as bad as I did.

Finally, I headed for the dressing rooms. To the right was the joyful, noisy celebrations of the Argentinians. I turned left. I knew this was going to be the hardest part, far harder than the TV interview I had just done, and far, far harder than saying 'Well done' to Passarella. What could I say? What could I say to players who had put every ounce of effort into the game, only to go out in such a way? I don't think it would have been so hard had we been beaten, say, 4–2, but to play for so long with ten men, and play so well and have all those decisions go against us ... how do you pick people up after that? The reality is that there is very little you can say. Thank goodness that once we were inside our dressing room we couldn't hear the Argentinians. That would have been even worse.

There was silence in the dressing room. Total, absolute silence. I was aware of David Beckham sitting there. But it wasn't the time to talk to him. Eventually, I said, 'You've given absolutely everything out there. You did everything you could. The decisions went against you and I'm not going to stand here blaming anybody. Each one of you, when you walk out of that door, should put your chest out, put your chin up and walk out with pride.'

After that a few people started talking. John said a few words to certain players along the same lines. 'You couldn't have done any more,' I heard him saying. But there was still a lot of silence after that. It lasted for some time. I was vaguely aware of our media relations manager Steve Double coming in and saying something about a shirt to exchange, and about a row outside involving some TV people who were apparently being totally insensitive to the situation. But I took no notice. All I was worried about was how my players and my staff were coping.

I went round them individually. I shook them by the hand. I thanked them for the great effort they'd put in. I especially remember talking to Martin Keown and Les Ferdinand who were sitting next to each other. I went up to both of them and shook their hands. In many ways it had been harder for them since neither had been involved in the games. Les had reason to feel a bit resentful. After all, he'd been part of the Euro '96 squad without playing and now he hadn't been on the pitch at the World Cup. But I think he appreciated what I was saying. They were both experienced players who I'm sure would have played their part at some stage. Certainly, if we had played Holland, I would have detailed Martin (if he was fit) to play against Marc Overmars. But it was never to be and all I could say was that I knew about all the hard work they'd put in and that I could understand them feeling more gutted than the others, if that was possible.

Although there was silence in that dressing room, I could almost hear the emotion. I could almost hear the thoughts going through Tony Adams' mind, through Alan Shearer's mind, through young Michael Owen's mind, and through the minds of Les and Martin Keown. Alan Shearer sat naked on the floor for an unbelievable length of time. It was as if he couldn't actually bring himself to stand up and get on with his life.

David Batty was one of the first people to go into the shower. He didn't say anything, not like Tony Adams, who swore loudly as he went. David Beckham, meanwhile, had apparently gone round and apologized to the players, then talked to John and asked him to apologize to me. Emotions were flying high at that point and I don't think he felt like talking to me. Besides, I had another ordeal to face – a press conference, which frankly was the last thing in the world I felt like doing at that moment in time.

I knew that it would take days, months, perhaps years to come to terms with what had happened, but I also knew that elsewhere in the world there were earthquakes, deaths and births. This, for all its drama, was only football. Armed with that thought I finished going round the players, got changed, took a big breath and followed David Davies out of the door to go to talk to the press.

My resolve didn't last long. Within minutes I was really choked up again. Here I was walking out of that dressing room and into a TV interview with the BBC with who knows how many millions of people watching me. I was thinking, pull yourself together, because I was really close to tears at that point. What made it worse was that as I was walking out of the dressing room I saw Michelle Farrer and Joanne Budd from our media staff, sitting on the steps. I looked down at Michelle and she looked up at me. She'd been bawling her eyes out. I just gave her a kiss and had to choke back my own tears. She'd worked as hard as anyone for us. I gave Joanne a kiss, too. She just said, 'I'm so sorry.' Then, as I walked into the studio I saw Ray Stubbs. He was just about to interview me. He almost welled up. That was tough. We didn't say anything. We just embraced each other. For all the sadness, in many ways it was a wonderful moment.

Ray was really good. It was a delicate interview and he was very thoughtful. I tried to salvage something, anything ... but there was nothing to salvage. I'm sure the whole country was mourning at that time, and that nothing I said was going to make it any better. I just felt really sad sitting there and knowing how much effort we had all put in to no avail. I was still in shock.

After I'd done my interview with Ray, FIFA wanted me in

the mixed-zone press conference as quickly as possible. It was never going to be easy, but was made ten times worse by the fact that Daniel Passarella was still in there talking as I walked in. So back to the dressing room I went. David Davies told the FIFA officials to let us know when they were really ready. After a few minutes, they called us in a second time. When we returned, there were five Argentinian players up on the podium talking to the press. David blew his top at the FIFA officials while I stood and talked to the English press in a small area off to the side. Some of the questions were very to the point. They were bound to be – about David Beckham, about practising penalties, etc. Other questions, probably more than I'd expected, were sympathetic. Eventually, I went to the podium and talked briefly to the foreign press. It was all very disjointed, the worst press event of the tournament for us.

The dressing room, when I returned, was an eerie place. The masseurs were packing up and all the kit was being loaded for departure. Just about everyone else had gone too. It was a hard place to be. My next thought was for our families and friends. Where were they? In order to find them, I had to walk through the press conference again. As politely as I could, I declined yet more interviews. The only thing I did do was shake hands with an English woman who I'd originally mistaken for a foreign journalist. I had walked past her at first, but when I realized that she just wanted to shake hands, I returned. 'You were unlucky,' she said with a smile. 'You couldn't have done any more.'

Then a very strange thing happened. I arrived by the side of our team coach where the players, staff and families had gathered. Just at that moment I saw another coach drawing away. I thought it was full of Argentinian fans because they were singing the same song that the fans had been singing before the game, and swinging their shirts around their heads in the same way. They were at the window goading our players.

I thought to myself, 'That's all we need.' I didn't realize until a few minutes later that it wasn't a coach full of Argentinian fans ... it was the Argentinian players' coach. I was outraged. It was insensitive and unprofessional. Our players would never have done anything like that in a million years. It was a sporting event and we had tried to approach it as such. What they did was disgusting.

I walked off and I found my family after that. It was an emotional time. I remember my uncle whispering in my ear, 'You should be proud of what you've achieved. You'd have gone on and won it if you'd won that game,' he said. I can remember what he said word for word. My wife Anne was there too. I felt very, very sad for her. What was going on in our personal lives really hit me then. She was very strong, and put on a really brave face. The two kids had been crying. I hadn't seen them for so long that I just wanted to kiss and cuddle them. Jamie wouldn't let me put him down. Zara had painted the St George's flag on her nails. She told me she'd been crying ever since the Argentinians had scored their first goal, even though Jamie had tried to cheer her up. 'Don't cry Zara,' he'd apparently said. 'It's only a game.' That made me chuckle. Jamie didn't seem able to take it all in so I just kept cuddling him. Bless him. I saw Dave Deller, too. He was gutted for me and for everyone. There were plenty of tears.

The team flew back to St Nazaire that night. In the coach I remember sitting with John in the front and just embracing him. There wasn't much we could say to each other. We were such close friends, more than just number one and number two. Peter Taylor and Ray Clemence sitting on our left just looked numb. All the staff were too. We all just sat there for ages not saying anything. No music. No conversation. Just silence.

I didn't sleep on the flight. I just shut my eyes, but every time I did I just replayed the game in my mind. I said some prayers and I spent some time trying to come to terms with what had happened, trying to understand it. My uncle had been right. I couldn't get away from my belief that we'd have won the World Cup if we'd have beaten Argentina, and no-one on this earth will ever change my opinion that if we'd had eleven men on the pitch we'd have won that game. That's what really cut me up. I had told the players before the tournament that we were going to win it. I had told them we were going all the way. We went out there prepared for seven games, and I really felt we had a group of talented people working hard enough to go that far. We could have achieved so much, but we would never know just how much.

It was around 3 a.m. by the time we got back to La Baule. This time a huge flag said simply: 'Welcome Home'. The players had some food and a drink but the atmosphere was sad. The show was over. I had slept well throughout our World Cup campaign but I knew that sleep would probably be beyond me this time.

PART
THREE

CHAPTER 13

COMING HOME

1 JULY 1998

No-one likes to lose, but it wasn't until I was finally alone in my room at 4.45 a.m. on Wednesday 1 July that I realized just how much the defeat against Argentina had hurt. It was the most painful defeat I had suffered in all my years as a player and manager. Our World Cup adventure had ended in the cruellest way imaginable. And for the first time in the three weeks since we had arrived in France, sleep was beyond me. I dozed. I turned the TV on and off. Every channel seemed to be replaying the game over and over. Having briefly caught a phone-in in which a few callers were slagging us off, I have to admit that I found myself wondering whether I really needed the job of England coach any more. The feeling eventually passed.

I know that some of the players didn't get to bed at all that night. Alan Shearer, my captain, was one of them. At 7.30 a.m. he, Tim Flowers and a few others played the two or three holes of the golf course that backed on to the hotel. It was their way of coping with their bitter disappointment, their way of killing time until our flight home that afternoon, their way of avoiding having to think about what had happened. It hurt too much.

Brian Scott had had arrangements in place for us to fly home that Wednesday for a long time. He wasn't tempting fate; he had to be prepared. Like all of us, he never wanted the flight to be confirmed. But it had been, we were to take a flight at 3.15 p.m. from Nantes to Heathrow on a special British Airways charter. However, during the morning there was a change of plan. BA's chief executive had offered us Concorde if we wanted it, though the take-off would be forty-five minutes later than planned. When Brian rang me in my room, I told him, 'Just do it.'

The Prime Minister rang as well. It was an unexpected call and I had to rush out of the shower to talk to him. It was an uplifting chat, just as it was when we had talked at the start of the tournament. He's easy to talk to. I don't think he even minded me calling him Tony. He told me how proud the nation was of our performance. I told him that we had given it everything, and that I just felt let down by some of the referee's decisions. I said I was sure we could have gone on and won the World Cup and that I was disappointed that we would never now find out what this group of people could have achieved.

Graham Kelly and David Davies were in the room with me while I was speaking to the Prime Minister. I don't know why Graham was there. Maybe it was just his way of letting me know The F.A. was backing me all the way. He didn't actually come out and say it. He didn't need to.

At noon we had scheduled what was to be our last press conference at the media centre in L'Escoublac. The questions were predictable. Shouldn't we have practised penalties? Wasn't it a mistake not playing Michael Owen from the start of the tournament? Would I have done anything differently given the chance again? I'd wondered in advance what the main subject would be – was my job on the line? Are you going to quit? In fact, it soon became clear that the journalists really wanted to talk about David Beckham. However, I was determined to stress that David shouldn't be made a scapegoat for what happened. A red card, I said, had been a harsh punishment for his crime but he would have to live with it and we would support him – after all, England needs its best young players. I also made the point that we had done a lot right. Of course we had learned some lessons, but we were going home with our heads held high.

My voice was struggling at the start. An hour and a half – and thousands of words – later I was virtually speechless. On the way out of the conference a BBC journalist wanted to speak to David Davies and me privately. The *Mirror* had asked her whether she wanted to complain about me calling her 'love' live on TV during the press conference. It was pitiful considering I didn't even know I'd done it. Naturally I apologized to her and she said it hadn't upset her at all.

Back at the hotel, our bags were packed and lined up outside the entrance. We had photos taken with the hotel staff and then there was a presentation to the Doc on his retirement. John Gorman, who loves his drawings and is very good at them, had sketched a special portrait for him. There were farewells, and more than a few more tears. We hadn't prepared for this.

Somehow, it felt right travelling home on Concorde. I spoke to David Beckham on the journey. We stood together in the middle of the plane and chatted quietly. He apologized to me for his actions the previous night. I told him how pleased I was that he'd said that, and I also told him this had to be the end of the line for him as far as learning lessons was concerned. We'd warned him at Le Tournoi a year ago about getting involved with silly antics, but he obviously hadn't learned. He'd had no need to do what he did, even if the red card was harsh. If he hadn't got sent off we'd have had eleven men on the pitch and would have won the game – I was convinced of that. I also told him that I'd done my best to avoid putting a greater burden on his shoulders by naming scapegoats; that he was a special talent who was young enough to play in another World Cup; and that I was there for him in the future, as was his club. He said very little in reply. He didn't need to. I believe he got the message.

As Concorde touched down at the same Heathrow engineering terminal we'd left so full of hope twenty-two days before, the sight through the windows was spectacular. Several thousand people, many of them waving flags and banners, were applauding even before the plane came to a halt. Michael Owen accepted the pilot's invitation to sit in the cockpit as he brought the plane down, and once we'd landed the St George flag was hung out of the cockpit window. It made me wonder what would have happened had we brought the World Cup home.

As each player went down the steps of the plane, the cheers could be heard by all the coaches and the staff still waiting to disembark. It was emotional; it brought a lump to my throat. You never quite know how people back home might react to everything but I was left in no doubt by the massive cheer that went up when John and I emerged. It was an amazing feeling. As I went down the steps I started to wave. I didn't really know what I should do. People had been coming up to me and saying, 'Congratulations', but I didn't really feel it was the right word. 'Bad luck' or 'You were unlucky' might have been more appropriate, although I'd rather have been a lucky winner than an unlucky loser. So as I walked across the tarmac to the team bus, I threw my arms out wide as if to say, 'I don't think we could have done any more, certainly against Argentina.' I remember squeezing

John's shoulders … I wanted him to feel part of it. It had been a massive effort by all concerned.

More well-wishers lined the route to the Sheraton hotel where our luggage was to be handed out. They were very proud moments, but tinged with sadness as I reflected on how cruel football can be, not just to players and coaches, but to all those who had kicked every ball with us back home. For a split second I wondered again about wanting this job, but a split second was all it was.

At that hotel I said goodbye to every single member of our 'team' – players and staff. I tried to thank them all for what they had done. I told the players to have a good rest; I knew many of them were going straight off on holiday. Alan Shearer and Rob Lee were flying to Barbados with their families, while Becks had made special arrangements with his agent to fly straight on to America to be reunited with Victoria.

Eventually, John, Ray Cousins and I were the last people left. We drove out of the hotel past more cheering and clapping and headed for the M4. I looked at my appointments diary in my pocket. I'd lost all track of time. It was Wednesday 1 July. The pages were blank. I had nothing planned. 'I shouldn't be here,' I thought. It was a weird feeling. John said he felt the same – in limbo, at a loose end. If only we could have woken up and found ourselves still in the World Cup after all.

I embraced John when we dropped him at his home, then dropped my luggage off. Straight away, I headed round to see my children. It was strange, getting back into my own car for the first time in weeks and driving myself.

When I got there, a massive England flag was hanging from one of the bedroom windows. England scarves were draped all over the place. It was fantastic to see the children. I gave them each a big kiss and cuddle. Jamie wanted to play football as soon as I saw him. 'Dad,' he said, 'in the garden. I want to play golden goals and penalties. You're David Seaman and I'm Ronaldo.' At that moment the World Cup seemed a million miles away. Winning it remained what it had always been: a dream. My dream.

CHAPTER 14

RECOVERY

2 – 13 JULY 1998

The days following our return to England were terrible. My emotions were really mixed up. I found myself asking the same question again and again: 'Why am I here?'

I learnt many things over the course of our World Cup adventure; among them, that the World Cup is one of the biggest global events – and I don't just mean sporting events. It's so much bigger than the European Championships or the Olympic Games, or any political event I can think of. France '98 proved that. It was a fantastic tournament, despite what happened to us. Many of the matches were really exciting, classics even. And our exploits really brought the country together.

However, if the World Cup as a whole brought people together, in one respect it had the opposite effect. Some of the reaction to David Beckham's sending off illustrated that. You know the hype has gone too far when you see a picture of

David with a noose around his neck in a leading tabloid newspaper. That's frightening. It's a monster that we've got to control. Murderers have been treated better than David, yet he's just a young footballer. The reaction was so far over the top. What if David was your son or your brother? He's a human being and he doesn't deserve the treatment some lunatics are threatening at their grounds in the new season. The injustice of it disgusts me. It's something we need to address as a nation. A line must be drawn.

To be honest, I think David may need someone outside football to help him get through the next few months. Counselling of some sort would help, perhaps from Eileen Drewery. Ironically, I had spoken to David just before we left for France and warned him that, with Gazza out of the squad, he might be the next target. Even then I saw the danger signs. I was aware that he might need help, without really knowing what was going to happen. I think he now needs it more than ever.

All of us who care about football have got to look seriously at David's situation. We've made progress in many parts of the game – in fighting hooliganism inside the grounds, and against racism. Football's image is on the up. Now there's a chance for fans to show that that new image actually means something. It's a chance for real supporters to show compassion and forgiveness. I can; can they?

It's a test for the whole nation. If you've never made a mistake in your life you might think you're justified in crucifying David, but you're not. He will have learnt a big enough lesson without having to carry this terrible emotional burden on his shoulders everywhere he goes.

If it does get too bad he could even think of going abroad, which is something we really don't want our most talented young English players to do. We are losing a lot of English players through foreign ones coming into our game as it is. But something like this may leave a deep scar, and I know

David needs support and help. Let's just hope the football public really has changed. The last thing anyone wants is for him to be driven out.

On a purely footballing front I couldn't bring myself to watch the first of the quarter-finals after our arrival home. But I have to admit that I really enjoyed seeing Holland beat Argentina, particularly after the way the Argentinians had behaved as they drove out of the car park in St Etienne. I saw what that did to our players.

I watched the game with my dad. We were both out of our seats as the story unfolded from Marseilles. Dennis Bergkamp's was a marvellous winning goal and it was sweet seeing it hit the back of the net. It's amazing how it all unfolds, as Bergkamp really shouldn't have been playing. He ought to have been sent off for stamping on a Yugoslav player in their second-round match. But I do love the way the Dutch play their total football. Their goalkeeper – Van Der Saar – is like a second sweeper; he starts off all their attacks. Whether they can ever win a tournament playing that way I don't know. They are at the stage Brazil were at between 1970 and 1990 when they had to change their philosophy to win a World Cup. The Dutch are wonderful to watch, probably wonderful to play for – but not bad to play against, either. I would have loved to have had that challenge. I would have fancied us to win. It's all ifs and buts now though.

Seeing my family and friends, relating my World Cup story to them, and hearing theirs, helped me cope in the days after we returned from France. At least I had managed to sleep, unlike my mum, who didn't sleep for four nights after we lost to Argentina. I visited my cousin Michelle, baby Deon and dad, Olly, who were doing well, and of course I saw Vanessa. But I felt very emotional in many ways. I also had to deal with my personal situation which was on hold throughout the World Cup. It had been put in a box which I now had to open. It hit me hard.

The children were great. They really cheered me up. I spent time playing football with Jamie on my first weekend back in England. It might sound like the last thing I needed, but it was actually a great release, a way of getting back on track. When I went to Jamie's sports day, lots of mothers came up and told me what the World Cup had meant to them, even though none of them had ever watched football before.

But I'd be lying if I said I didn't find it hard to get over the experience. It was an emotional rollercoaster. One moment I was making all those decisions in France every day ... then boom, it was over. But I know that there are much, much bigger issues in life. The three children who were burnt to death in their own home in Northern Ireland over the weekend of the World Cup Final put it all into perspective for me. I felt so badly for them and their family.

I was committed to work for ITV for the duration of the Finals once we were out of the competition, but I was dreading it. Eventually, however, I faced up to it and went to Marseilles for the Brazil–Holland semi-final. It turned out to be a positive step towards my recovery. I also got a very up beat reaction to England's performance from the foreign journalists and TV people I met there. My fellow ITV panellists – Kevin Keegan, Ruud Gullit and Terry Venables – were sympathetic as well. I saw Alex Ferguson there but we avoided talking about David Beckham. Neither he nor I brought the subject up. It wasn't the time or the place.

At the Final in Paris, I had five minutes to myself inside the Stade de France just before the national anthems. Five minutes to take everything in. Reality hit me, and it hurt. It brought a lump to my throat. I thought of what might – and should – have been. Our supporters should have been filling the stadium. Our players should have been down on the pitch lining up. My staff should have been sitting on the bench, and 'God Save The Queen' should have been blaring out.

I had a strange feeling France would beat Brazil that night. I predicted as much, and for someone who is renowned as a hopeless gambler it was a pretty good call. They were the team who had enjoyed much of the good fortune going throughout the tournament, against the likes of Paraguay, Italy and Croatia. I was really pleased for their coach Aimé Jacquet after all the flak he'd taken over the past couple of years, and for Gerard Houllier, a great friend of mine who has had a big input in French football over the last six years. I'm thrilled he's gone to Liverpool where he will be working with some of our English players. I was also delighted for the French full-back, Lillian Thuram. When I was recovering from my knee injury at Monaco, he was a sixteen year old suffering from a similar, but apparently more serious, problem. A physio had told him he wouldn't play again. Of course he did, and it was great to see him star in a World Cup Final.

But it was more than just good fortune which won France the World Cup. Over the years they've always had tremendous flair but they've lacked the physical presence to complement it, as well as the mental belief that they were good enough to be world champions. Over the last six years they've evolved into a team that has it all, with players like Desailly and Blanc at the back, and Deschamps in midfield. A great deal was spoken about Zidane and he is a wonderful player, but you can't say he had a wonderful tournament. Granted, he had a fantastic final: he scored twice and played extremely well in the first forty-five minutes, but does that make him a world-class player and one of the all-time greats? I'm not sure.

Everything went France's way on the night. Brazil never had a chance once it was clear that Ronaldo shouldn't have been on the pitch. He was limping, hobbling even, and wasn't even looking to find the spaces he normally does. In the studio, Ruud, Terry and I were all flabbergasted. I'm not sure we'll ever know the full story but I really hope it wasn't football giving in to commercial pressures to play him. It underlines just how much pressure there is in the modern game and how vigilant we will have to be with Michael Owen.

The injury aside, I think Ronaldo missed Romario during the tournament. They'd played together up front for game after game in the friendly matches and suddenly, at the crucial moment, Romario suffered an injury that ruled him out. I think that was a significant blow to Ronaldo. It also left Zagallo having to find a new striking partnership at the eleventh hour. He never succeeded. Also, I was never convinced that Brazil could sustain the momentum over seven games, and it panned out that way. It was interesting that Dunga had to play every game; it suggests that Zagallo felt that no-one else could fill the role of playmaker. That's a position where Brazil have changed. They played a European-style player in that role, one who understands the game but who sometimes lacks the flair that has always characterized Brazil. The Brazilians were exciting at times, but they never really took off in the way that people had hoped.

After the match, ITV threw a party for the commentator Brian Moore to celebrate his retirement. He'll be sadly missed. I remember him interviewing me when I was a seventeen year old at Tottenham and I have a lot of respect for him. He's a very humble man who has achieved a great deal. There was talk at the party about a horrible newspaper article about Brian in the *Independent* which, at the end of his career, couldn't find a good thing to say about him. He was upset by it. We all were. I have absolutely no idea what purpose articles like that serve. The Brian Moore I know wound up his career by saying that the important thing that night was that France had won the World Cup. He bowed out with a touch of class.

The French paraded the trophy on the Champs-Elysées the day after their triumph and millions of people turned out to celebrate. It should have been us coming down the Mall towards Buckingham Palace. That had been planned.

I was over the worst by this time though. I had even started planning for our first European Championship qualifying match in Sweden in September. Football never stops.

But first of all I needed a holiday.

CHAPTER 15

ASSESSMENT

England didn't qualify for the World Cup Finals in America in 1994. But since then we reached the last four at Euro '96, which was a tribute to the players, Terry Venables and his staff. We topped a very difficult qualifying group to make it to the 1998 World Cup. At France '98, we reached the last sixteen and should have gone further. I believe that had we beaten Argentina, we would have won the World Cup. There is a widespread belief, and not just at home, that we have a squad that can go on to greater things. They've had the unbelievable experience of France '98. They've discovered levels of fitness they probably never knew they had. They are among the favourites for Euro 2000. This is the good news. The bad news, of course, is that it didn't happen for us in France. For the third time in eight years, England went out of a major tournament on penalties. Should we have practised them more? Can you ever practise anything too much?

Of course we put in a certain amount of practice. But you can never recreate on the training ground the circumstances of a real shoot-out. I know – I've taken penalties in Cup finals. That walk from the halfway line to the penalty spot, with millions of eyes upon you, is when it hits you. When you run up, and that goal starts shrinking, then you know you're in trouble. Unfortunately you don't know how you are going to feel until that moment of truth. Frankly, you've either got it, or you haven't.

From the coach's perspective, picking your penalty takers in advance isn't necessarily that clever either. As my experience with David Beckham showed, you don't always know who's going to be on the pitch at the end of the game. Not only that, but some players are quite open about not wanting to take – or even practise – penalties.

The unfortunate thing is that I think England's footballers now have a big psychological block to overcome when it comes to penalty shoot-outs. (The same goes for Italy – they suffered the same fate in 1990, 1994 and 1998.) Practising until kingdom come isn't necessarily the answer. In fact, it might just make things worse; we don't want to build an even higher mental wall. Of course, it's my job to come up with the answer, and it needs a lot of thought.

My own theory, and it's a good time to say it, is that penalties should be taken at the end of ninety minutes, and before extra-time and any golden goal. It would still be exciting, but it would be fairer. The team losing the penalty shoot-out would know that with time running out, they must score; in pressing forward for a possible winner they may give the opposition the chance to break away and finish things off. Either way, it finishes as a football test for players and coaches. It doesn't end with the hopes of millions of people resting on one person and his state of mind on that walk from the halfway line to the penalty spot.

In St Etienne, Michael Owen put his penalty away as well

as anybody. I think the way we handled him in France was spot on. He was one of the stars of the tournament, and deservedly so. He's a very mature, sensible lad with a fantastic future. What's happened to him already is a tribute to him and his family, but I like to think that we've played a part. Yet people still ask, shouldn't we have played him from the start of the tournament rather than breaking him in gradually as we did?

That first game in Marseilles against Tunisia was always going to be the most tense, and in some ways most important one of our campaign. I picked what I considered to be a balanced team to start, first against Tunisia, then against Romania. We knew both teams would play with deep-lying sweepers. We knew the track record and experience of Alan Shearer and Teddy Sheringham together – remember all those headlines about football's SAS – and with Paul Scholes in the side as well, we were always going to start the tournament that way.

Just supposing Michael had started against Tunisia, hadn't scored, and I'd had to take him off. Given that scenario, I don't think he'd have emerged as he did – with flying colours. As it was, the way we brought him on took the pressure off him and gave him the best chance to produce his top form.

Anyway, we beat Tunisia with a good performance, and if we hadn't made those defensive mistakes I think we'd have done for Romania as well. But we always intended to start Michael against Colombia. Playing as they did, with a flat back four, they were vulnerable to the ball over the top and we knew a partnership of Shearer and Owen would give them real problems.

The truth is that having selected the youngest player in the history of English football to be part of a World Cup squad, I've no regrets about the way we handled him and brought him on.

With regard to our second-round match, I said at the time

that Argentina suited us better as our opponents than Croatia and I meant it. Of course we tried to win our group – you'd expect nothing else from professional footballers – but I prepared for both countries as potential opponents.

Croatia would have proved a bigger struggle. Their coach, Blazevic, did a wonderful job keeping them focused and channelling their patriotism in the right direction. They must now be among the favourites for Euro 2000. I knew all about players like Suker, Boban and Prosinecki, but I wasn't sure whether they could get their balance right game after game during the tournament. In the end, of course, they did. In fact, they ended up in the semi-finals and claimed third place. However, at the time they were more of an unknown quantity and the nation would probably have expected us just to put the shirts on and turn up to beat them. We risked no such complacency among the public and press with Argentina.

David Beckham and Michael Owen could not have had more contrasting experiences in France '98. It certainly wasn't the way I wanted to be proved right, but I have to say that what happened against Argentina vindicated my judgement that David wasn't properly focused on the task early on in the tournament. He needed a jolt, and he got it. He responded in the best way possible against Romania and then Colombia, but appeared to take a step backwards in what turned out to be our last match. There's no way he'd have even thought of doing what he did against Argentina if his mind had been 100 per cent focused.

It's been even harder to take on the chin what I consider to be another mistake – the referee's decision not to give us a penalty in extra-time against Argentina when their defender clearly handled the ball when he went up with Alan Shearer. If the referee says it was accidental, then what on earth was that defender's hand doing above Alan's head in the first place? It was a decision that really cost us.

I think he didn't give it because he had already given two penalties. A third – and the golden goal that would surely have followed – was one too many for him. I'm not sure many referees would want to give a penalty in the golden-goal period of any match. For me though, looking back, it was the decisive moment. You don't expect every decision to go your way but you do need the key ones to.

What made things worse was that through a crowded penalty area, the same referee had managed to see Alan's 'foul' on their goalkeeper that denied Sol Campbell the winner in normal time. The referee also gave David Beckham a red card when I'm sure many others would have pulled out a yellow. I'm not blaming the referee, though. I know the pressure he was under and I'm convinced his were honest decisions. But I also know how I saw them.

Overall though, I think the referees coped very well with the new directives on the tackle from behind. We were all very sceptical when the new rules came out but our fears proved unfounded, even though there were a few occasions when I expected a red card that never arrived. I did feel, however, that the referees were looking to stamp their authority on a game early on by issuing a yellow card for a trivial offence, which then meant the culprit was on thin ice for the rest of the game. Inevitably, there were a lot of players sent off for a second bookable offence, which effectively ended the games concerned as contests.

One of the biggest negatives to come out of the tournament was that too many players seemed to be encouraged by the new directives to get their opponents booked by diving. It's a habit that is creeping into the game and one that should be stamped out fast. It's a challenge to the game's rulers to come up with a solution.

Naturally I've been asked if I would do anything differently if I had my time again. Well, you learn from your experiences as much as anything else, and the answer to the question is yes.

Of course, if I'd known that David Seaman was going to make an early save in the penalty shoot-out, giving us the chance to take the lead, I'd have had one of our experienced penalty takers at number two in the order.

There was definitely a lesson to be learned from the goals we gave away through lack of concentration in defence. As coach, I must find a way of ensuring those lapses aren't repeated. At international level, you can't afford to switch off in games, even for a second.

I really would hold my hands up and admit to being wrong if I thought I'd mishandled either David Beckham or Michael Owen. But I think events proved me right. As for Gazza, I made my assessment of his fitness levels and that was that. Say we'd had to battle for an hour and a quarter with ten men as we did against Argentina and Gazza had been on the pitch. With his level of fitness, I think we'd have been in big trouble.

In contrast, most of our players said they'd never felt as strong or as fit as they were at France '98. There was a lot of nonsense written about our use of food and vitamin supplements like creatine after we came home. The fact is that other countries have taken them for years. They're not illegal. Taken over short periods of time, and not in excess, there's no evidence to suggest they are in any way harmful. It's insulting to our medical staff to suggest they'd ever do anything that risked hurting our players.

What was written about creatine was almost as silly as the suggestion that Paul Ince had played through the World Cup with a broken ankle. That was nonsense, too. I saw the X-ray with my own eyes, which I like to do for my own education. It's true that Incey had been injured in an end-of-season clash with Ian Wright, of all people, in a Liverpool–Arsenal match at Anfield. But that injury to his ankle steadily improved over the weeks leading up to and during the tournament. The X-ray showed up an old injury that was really a chipped bone in the same ankle. There was no more to it than that. If ever a story was exaggerated to sell papers, that was it.

The biggest mistake I think I made was in not getting Eileen Drewery out to join us from the start. All her flights and accommodation were sorted out for after the Argentina match. It was too late. A lot of the players wanted – and needed – to see her. There was both physical and mental healing to be done. The stresses and strains of the World Cup were taking their toll and Eileen would have helped ease them. The coach is probably the last person players will share those stresses and strains with; his deputy – John Gorman in my case – the second-last person. Their anxieties are best shared with someone else who they can trust. Eileen has that gift.

The reason I didn't get her out to France earlier was that I knew she had important commitments of her own at home. But I know that if I had asked her to come out then she would have responded positively. I regret it in a big way. She could have helped me as well, as she did when we returned. It was a huge shock to me that we didn't beat Argentina, and didn't win the World Cup. I needed her help, as much as that of my family, to get over it.

Having said all that, we didn't have one major problem with a player or member of the staff during the World Cup; no discipline problems, no rows in training, no staff dis-agreements. I couldn't have asked for better. When I needed to give the subs a bit of a boost I trained with them myself. It made me laugh when I trained with them after the Romania defeat and somebody wrote that I looked dishevelled and under pressure at the press conference that followed. You'd have looked the same if you'd had Steve McManaman run-ning at you for almost an hour in the heat!

I know that the press keep saying that I select the team,

then try to keep it inside the camp. They say I'm too secretive, that it's wrong to throw them a few googlies. But I say it's just being professional. I didn't see too many other coaches naming their teams days in advance and giving their opponents time to work on tactics. But the media – or at least those who've chosen not to understand – think I'm trying to pull the wool over their eyes. I wouldn't be so stupid. I'm just doing my best for our players and our team. My target is to try to deceive our opponents if I can. If I know for certain the players in the opposing team, then I know their shape and I know who will be marking who. There's no other reason for my actions.

Having not read most of the press during the World Cup, I can't give an opinion on what they wrote overall. All I can say is that I quite enjoyed most of our news conferences. I thought the majority of the questions were fair, and there were some light-hearted moments, too.

I've got to be optimistic about the players who came through so much in France and emerged from the tournament with their reputations enhanced. Michael Owen's name is now known around the world. That goal of his against Argentina gets more sensational every time I think about it. The experience he gained at France '98 will have lifted his self-belief still higher than it was at the start. The 1998–9 season could be a difficult one for him with all the hype there's been, but he'll handle it. He's got that maturity, he's got his family behind him and Liverpool is a good club when it comes to keeping players' feet on the ground; certainly the Anfield fans will help. We still need to work on his left side and on his heading so that he can become an even better player.

Like Michael, I think Sol Campbell will be a big influence on the England scene for years to come. He has always been a magnificent defender. We've worked on his technical skills with plenty of ballwork at all our training sessions. He's really flourished. Like Michael, I think he really believes in himself now. His natural foot is his right one, but he played very successfully down the left channel for us. He'll get better and better I'm sure.

Paul Scholes will get that self-belief as well. He's a terrific little player who I hope gets a full season with his club. He needs games regularly and he'll always score goals for you if you play him in the right positions.

My captain, Alan Shearer, remains the best striker in England at the moment. It's a thrilling prospect for all of us that both he and Michael Owen can still be together at another World Cup. Of course I would have liked us to have created more chances for Alan in France. But they fell to others. We all know Alan's reputation worldwide.

What's really good is that, unlike some other countries, we've now got so many young players who've got World Cup experience. Are they world-class players? I think that tag comes when you win something at international level. Michael Owen, Scholesy, Sol, Gary Neville, David Beckham, Rio Ferdinand and others can make it, given time.

Tony Adams may find 2002 a tournament beyond him, but he can still be part of Euro 2000. He was so important to us. We nursed him through to France although I had to plan how to do without him. Having him was a massive bonus.

What he achieved was a lesson for so many other players. Everything he's experienced – how he's changed, what made him change and how he came through – should be passed on to every young player we've got.

I now see Tony stretch, and do things on the pitch he couldn't do at twenty and twenty-one because of the way he was handling his life. I played with him myself many years ago, people forget that. Now I talk to him and he's a different person altogether. He's cut out all his bad habits so he's fitter and leaner. His physical and mental approach has changed, and therefore so has he. He's done a fantastic job for England, which was why I felt really sad for him in the dressing room in St Etienne.

Gazza needs to look at what Tony has achieved. I had to take a tough decision about him which deep in his heart I think he knows was right. The door hasn't been slammed in his face for good. He's got to change drastically though and get fitter than he's ever been in his life. Sure he'll have a few blinding club games, and people will say, 'How can Hoddle leave him out?' But for him to play for England over the next two years, he's got to avoid injuries. He'll have a much better chance of doing that if he's mentally fitter and stronger. He's got to get rid of so much of the mental baggage he continues to carry around with him. He's got to change his habits off the pitch. He's got to sort out his drinking, he's got to have the right diet. At his age, that's a massive challenge. But can he do it? Has he got the right people around him he can do it with?

Only Paul knows the answers. If he succeeds, and I hope he does, he still has the chance of playing international football. We'll be watching over the first few months of the 1998–9 season when he's back in the Premiership. It's a big, big season for Gazza.

As for my own future, I've made it clear that I intend to see out my contract, and that means taking England to Euro 2000 in Holland and Belgium. I want to stay for that. I want to give it a good shot. I can't say beyond that but I can say that it will have nothing to do with money. Before I went to Chelsea I could have got three times the salary elsewhere. I could earn much more than I do now.

After coming back from France I was offered the coaching job at Real Madrid. Monaco would, of course, be an interesting proposition if it came up and the timing was right. I know people there and it's a special place to me. But the timing isn't right.

Over the next few months I'll talk to people and come to a decision. I know Graham Kelly wants to talk to me, but it's too soon to rush into anything. This job is huge; even Tony Blair told me he didn't envy my task. He told me he thought it was a worse job than his for the five weeks' duration of a tournament like the World Cup.

I can't look as far ahead as the World Cup of 2002 at the moment. I was filling the car up at a garage the other day when a man came up to me. He said, 'You've done fantastic. Stay and win it the next time.' It hit me hard as he walked away. The prospect of a European team trying to win four years from now in Japan and Korea is an exciting one. Do I want to wait that long to bury the ghost, to achieve the dream?

I have to decide what I want to do with my life. At the moment I don't think I'll stay in football for the next twenty years. I'm not the English Zagallo who'll be around for ever, that's for sure. I see my life going in another direction. Where? God only knows! Some people use that expression in a flippant way. It means a lot to me because there are some things in my life I hand over to my faith. Those who enjoy a relationship with God will understand that. I'm hoping I'll be shown where I'm meant to be going and what I'm meant to be doing. Perhaps it won't be what I want. But it will be what I need.

I'll get over what happened in France. I have to. But there will always be a scar, and I will always wonder what might have been. On Sunday 12 July at the Stade de France I looked at the French coach Aimé Jacquet. I was genuinely pleased for him. There was no envy. His had been a fantastic achievement. And yet I'll always believe it should have been me. It should have been England.